THE **COMPLETE**
IDIOT'S
GUIDE TO

Facebook
Marketing

by John Wayne Zimmerman and Damon Brown

ALPHA

A member of Penguin Group (USA) Inc.

ALPHA BOOKS

Published by the Penguin Group

Penguin Group (USA) Inc., 375 Hudson Street, New York, New York 10014, USA • Penguin Group (Canada), 90 Eglinton Avenue East, Suite 700, Toronto, Ontario M4P 2Y3, Canada (a division of Pearson Penguin Canada Inc.) • Penguin Books Ltd., 80 Strand, London WC2R 0RL, England • Penguin Ireland, 25 St. Stephen's Green, Dublin 2, Ireland (a division of Penguin Books Ltd.) • Penguin Group (Australia), 250 Camberwell Road, Camberwell, Victoria 3124, Australia (a division of Pearson Australia Group Pty. Ltd.) • Penguin Books India Pvt. Ltd., 11 Community Centre, Panchsheel Park, New Delhi—110 017, India • Penguin Group (NZ), 67 Apollo Drive, Rosedale, North Shore, Auckland 1311, New Zealand (a division of Pearson New Zealand Ltd.) • Penguin Books (South Africa) (Pty.) Ltd., 24 Sturdee Avenue, Rosebank, Johannesburg 2196, South Africa • Penguin Books Ltd., Registered Offices: 80 Strand, London WC2R 0RL, England

International Standard Book Number: 978-1-61564-154-3
Library of Congress Catalog Card Number: 2011936718

14 13 12   8 7 6 5 4 3 2

Interpretation of the printing code: The rightmost number of the first series of numbers is the year of the book's printing; the rightmost number of the second series of numbers is the number of the book's printing. For example, a printing code of 12-1 shows that the first printing occurred in 2012.

Printed in the United States of America

Note: This publication contains the opinions and ideas of its author. It is intended to provide helpful and informative material on the subject matter covered. It is sold with the understanding that the author and publisher are not engaged in rendering professional services in the book. If the reader requires personal assistance or advice, a competent professional should be consulted.

The author and publisher specifically disclaim any responsibility for any liability, loss, or risk, personal or otherwise, which is incurred as a consequence, directly or indirectly, of the use and application of any of the contents of this book.

Most Alpha books are available at special quantity discounts for bulk purchases for sales promotions, premiums, fundraising, or educational use. Special books, or book excerpts, can also be created to fit specific needs.

For details, write: Special Markets, Alpha Books, 375 Hudson Street, New York, NY 10014.

Publisher: *Marie Butler-Knight*

Associate Publisher/Acquiring Editor: *Mike Sanders*

Executive Managing Editor: *Billy Fields*

Development Editor: *Jennifer Moore*

Senior Production Editor: *Kayla Dugger*

Copy Editor: *Jan Zoya*

Cover Designer: *Kurt Owens*

Book Designers: *William Thomas, Rebecca Batchelor*

Indexer: *Angie Bess Martin*

Layout: *Brian Massey*

Proofreader: *John Etchison*

ALWAYS LEARNING

PEARSON

To Kimberly and Lucy —John
To Parul —Damon

Contents

Appendixes

Introduction

The idea of Facebook marketing seems odd, doesn't it? For most people, the social network seems like a way to connect awkwardly with high school friends or to see family pictures from relatives far away. However, a handful of businesses know the true power of Facebook. They know that reaching one influential person on the site could create the next viral sensation, bringing them both brand notoriety and significant revenue.

We'd like you to join this group. In the following pages, we show you how to attract a bigger audience, what to say to get your brand known, and why Facebook will soon be the most effective social media tool in your marketing arsenal. And, as with every book in this series, we do so with a level of clarity that will make even novices comfortable.

How This Book Is Organized

This book is divided into five main parts.

Part 1, Strategic Facebook Marketing, covers the basics, including your Facebook plan, how campaigns differ in the online world, and what you need to get your business page going. We tell you specific ways to integrate Facebook into your marketing plan, including determining cost effectiveness, your niche, and your public image/voice.

Part 2, Your Business on Facebook, explains the different types of business pages, how to build relationships, and what visitors you'd like to attract. Here you find out how to make your page from scratch, deciding between personal, Fan, and Group pages, and establishing a relationship with your customers using Facebook.

Part 3, Engaging Customers on Facebook, introduces ways you can keep visitors coming back for more, even after they've made a purchase. We include extensive discussions on viral videos and interactive games, which can bring people to your Facebook page, as well as curated News Feeds and fan maintenance, which can keep people coming back to your page.

Part 4, Facebook Measurement and Sales Tools, profiles the many, many ways the social network can help you track progress, market penetration, and sales. As we show in the chapters, Facebook provides lots of statistics for you to track the effectiveness of your campaign and cool tools, like Facebook Places, that can provide virtually free advertising for you and your business.

Part 5, Mastering Facebook, discusses the advanced ways you can make Facebook work for you. Once you've gotten the basics down, we show you ways to make an effective marketing team, find an effective consultant, and maintain and strengthen your business image on Facebook.

We also include appendixes for your reference. Appendix A is a glossary of common online marketing terms. Appendix B is a list of great books and online resources. If you need an overview of Facebook itself, Appendix C provides good stats on the popular social network. Finally, Appendix D is a quick checklist of what you need to prosper on Facebook.

Extras

There is always more to learn about online marketing. Each chapter in this book contains useful sidebars under the following headings:

DEFINITION

Check these sidebars for definitions of Facebook marketing words that may be unfamiliar to you.

FRIENDLY ADVICE

Here you'll find tips, hints, and insights to help you understand Facebook.

WATCH OUT

These are warnings about marketing strategies you'll want to avoid.

FEEDBACK

Check these sidebars for tidbits you may not have heard before.

Acknowledgments

John would like to thank his wife, Kimberly Ella, who has always supported him and taught him the meaning of unconditional love and friendship, his daughter, Lucy Love, who is his ultimate fan, and the many people in his personal and professional life who have encouraged him to live a life of truth, integrity, and passion.

Damon would like to thank his family, his fiancée, Dr. Parul Patel, John Wayne Zimmerman, and agent Marilyn Allen for bringing him to the project, media mavens Rachel Weingarten and Jennifer Abernethy, and the readers who have supported his previous books.

Trademarks

All terms mentioned in this book that are known to be or are suspected of being trademarks or service marks have been appropriately capitalized. Alpha Books and Penguin Group (USA) Inc. cannot attest to the accuracy of this information. Use of a term in this book should not be regarded as affecting the validity of any trademark or service mark.

Strategic Facebook Marketing

Sure, Facebook is social media, but many of the same marketing rules apply. Part 1 tells you how Facebook differs from traditional mediums, helps you define your target market, and shows you what you can do to keep them coming to your page. It also explains why having a Facebook presence today is just as important as having a website and how Facebook should be one of many ways you reach both your in-store and internet audiences.

Your Facebook Strategy

In This Chapter

- Harnessing the power of social networks
- Connecting with customers
- Setting realistic goals
- Creating successful social marketing campaigns
- Working with competitors

Facebook is one of the largest social networks in the world, connecting more than 800 million users. But with all those individuals, companies, and products vying for attention, how do you get the spotlight to shine on your business? In this chapter, we start the conversation by discussing what Facebook is, how you can use it to increase your business, and ways you can leverage Facebook in conjunction with other social networking tools.

Why You Need Facebook

Facebook gives businesses a great deal of advantages. Here are some of the biggest:

- Interacting directly with customers
- Promoting their brand more cheaply than through other mediums such as TV, radio, and print media
- Providing opportunities for ideas to go viral
- Enabling faster responses to feedback

These networks give small companies the leverage to make a significant impact, and they give large corporations the chance to move swifter through the marketplace.

And believe it or not, social network marketing is still in its infancy. Compare Facebook marketing, which is just a few years old, to promotion through television or radio. Because the rules aren't completely written, Facebook gives all of us an amazing opportunity to be innovative, groundbreaking, and, most importantly, successful.

Using Facebook, you can set up these marketing avenues for your business:

- A Profile page for your business

- Your virtual storefront

- Pages for sales and other promotions

It's All About the Customer

Facebook is different things to different people. For some individuals, it's a great way to connect with high school or college friends and family members. For others, it's a place to play games such as FarmVille and Bejeweled Blitz. And for many businesses, Facebook is a vast online marketplace where you have the potential to connect with millions of individuals for free.

However, your *social network* storefront needs a little TLC. The main thing you need to facilitate is a positive, responsive relationship with your customer.

DEFINITION

A **social network** is a website that enables people to connect with like-minded individuals and/or to support and learn about their favorite brands.

The best way to support your potential customer is by taking three steps:

1. Define your customers.

2. Find your customers.

3. Fulfill your customers' needs.

The following sections show you how.

Define Your Customers

First, you have to determine who your customers should be. You need to know who your potential customers are before you develop a marketing campaign to attract them. For instance, if you're going after a young, tech-savvy audience, they're already well-acquainted with Facebook, so your marketing campaign needs to get their attention in a fun, aggressive way. If you're going after an older, more conservative audience, your Facebook campaign needs to be more subtle.

You can even use Facebook to help you define your customers. For example, using Facebook statistics, you may find that more women than men like your business's Facebook page. That additional insight helps you better focus not only your Facebook marketing campaign, but your entire marketing plan.

FEEDBACK

Three Harvard students—Cameron and Tyler Winklevoss and Divya Narendra—claim that they came up with the original Facebook concept. They hired Mark Zuckerberg to create the website, but he reportedly stole the idea and built it for himself while stonewalling them. They reportedly found out when one of their girlfriends logged in to the site! The Winklevoss twins won a small payout in court, but sued again because they felt as though the compensation wasn't reflective of the company's worth. They lost.

Find Your Customers

After you identify your customers, you need to get them to your Facebook promotion. You can get potential customers to your Facebook page or Profile using the following techniques:

- Creating online events (see Chapter 11)
- Using viral media (see Chapter 12)
- Leveraging traditional marketing (see Chapter 3)
- Promoting well-branded games (see Chapter 13)

We go deeper into these and other opportunities later in the book.

Fulfill Your Customers' Needs

Smart marketing means nothing if the customer doesn't walk away satisfied. For one thing, you should want your customer to have a positive experience when dealing with your company. You want them to think you have a great product and a great relationship with your company. This desire for customer satisfaction goes beyond an inherent wish to treat people right. It's a good marketing tool. After all, customers talk! Even in the age of Facebook, word of mouth may still be the most powerful tool. In fact, Facebook is a word-of-mouth accelerant: whatever people used to talk about only at the coffee shops and the water cooler they now spread virtually—and at lightning speed—on social networks.

Define Your Business Goals

What, exactly, does a successful Facebook campaign mean? That's something you have to determine yourself. After all, how do you know if it's successful if you don't set solid goals and parameters? Even more than with other marketing strategies, it can be nearly impossible to know if a Facebook marketing plan is effective without definitive ideas of what success means.

Here are three steps to a realistic goal:

1. Determine all you want.

2. Prioritize your goals.

3. Measure your results.

What Do You Want?

This point is crucial: take your time and think about what your business wants or needs most from Facebook. Social networking can generate a litany of results, including the following:

- Higher sales

- Better brand recognition

- Appropriate platform for new product/service launch

- Greater revenue

WATCH OUT

Overambitious goals can be as destructive as not having any goals at all. If you have 5 percent of the market share and you want your Facebook campaign to garner more than half of the market share within a few months, you're probably setting yourself up for failure and frustration. Make small, specific goals.

Make your list of objectives as long as you like. Right now, you're just trying to list all the results you desire from Facebook marketing.

Prioritize

Prioritize your list of objectives in order of importance. It may seem obvious that certain goals supersede others, but prioritizing goals also helps you make quick decisions if the goals conflict.

For example, a Facebook marketing campaign may be great for an upcoming product launch, but doing your dream campaign may cost too much money. You need to make some hard decisions. Here are some questions to ask when your goals conflict:

- Is your company revenue solid enough for it to take a loss this year?

- Will the new product add more revenue in the long run?

- Can the campaign be spread across multiple products, not just the new one?

Answering these questions before beginning enables you to prioritize your goals and make effective decisions quickly.

Show Me the Money

No matter what your priorities, you need to be realistic about how much money you can put into your Facebook marketing campaign. We've seen too many businesses—both large and small—go way over their Facebook marketing budget.

The danger here is twofold. First, overextending your marketing money means that you may have to borrow against other, more important departments. Imagine having to cut production expenses to cover marketing, which could lead to shoddy products or, worse, not enough products.

Second, Facebook marketing takes time, so you want to make sure your money will last for several months. Facebook marketing is a commitment. Don't expect to throw up a Facebook page, watch it for a little while, and count the dollars. Think of your Facebook campaign as more of a marathon than a sprint. Budget your time, money, and energy carefully from the start.

Identifying Success

The following sections focus on issues you should consider as you look at the big-picture marketing plan.

Going Beyond the Numbers

It's easy to fall into the number game: "How many fans or *Likes* do you have on Facebook?" The more instructive question is this: how many of your fans do you actually interact with? To really understand the value of your Facebook marketing page, answer these questions:

- How much attention do you give to each customer?

- How quickly do you respond to a comment on Facebook?

- What do your most passionate fans get out of your Facebook page?

> **DEFINITION**
>
> When a Facebook user **Likes** your business page, product, event, or story, a "so-and-so likes your company" message appears on his Facebook Wall for all of his Facebook friends to see.

Use the answers to these questions to home in on what brings customers back. Accumulating more Likes is great, but you should make sure that you maintain a good relationship with the customers you currently have. We'll talk about this more in Chapter 9.

Campaign by Campaign

Not every marketing campaign should lead with Facebook. The social network isn't a one-size-fits-all site.

Let's say you're doing a campaign targeting musicians. Facebook may be the fastest-growing social network at the moment, but musicians still tend to prefer MySpace because it has the best music interface among the social networks. You might use

Facebook as a spoke within the campaign wheel, but you'll still want to base the entire hub of the campaign on MySpace because it has more of your desired audience.

> **WATCH OUT**
>
> It's easy to dismiss once-ubiquitous social networks like MySpace in favor of Facebook, but keep in mind that some social networks are more popular overseas. For instance, Hi5 (www.hi5.com) barely made a dent in America, but it's one of the largest social networks in Japan and Australia. Consider what your audience is using before limiting your social networking marketing strategy to Facebook.

That's the beauty of social networking: Facebook or any other social networking site can be the lead, or it can serve as the secondary or tertiary support within your marketing campaign.

Measure Success

How do you measure success? Here are some of the many ways to quantify your Facebook marketing's effectiveness:

- **Pure numbers:** Higher sales figures than the previous quarter.

- **Brand awareness:** Using studies to see how familiar people are with your company.

- **Customer interaction:** Seeing an increase or decrease in the number of people visiting your Facebook page (see Chapter 16).

In the end, only you can determine which stats are the most useful for showing you the effectiveness of your Facebook campaign. This book helps you determine the best one for your unique needs.

Observing the Competition

Getting involved with social networking was once considered cutting edge. Now? It's a necessity—just like having business cards or a website. Today, customers expect you to have a smart social networking plan that makes you look better than the competition. In other words, potential customers are evaluating your social networking savvy along with your product or service and considering how it stands up against the competition.

Finding Your Competition

One of the best ways to find your competition in the realm of social marketing is to do a search on Google for your service or product along with the term *Facebook*. For instance, Google "Facebook tires" and you'll see all the tire companies that have a significant presence on Facebook. Mind you, we didn't say the *biggest* tire companies on Facebook—the Goodyears, Firestones, and so on—but the ones with the biggest *presence* on Facebook.

Search engine optimization, online branding, and customer awareness are associated with websites, but they apply to Facebook, too.

> **DEFINITION**
>
> **Search engine optimization** (SEO) is the process of organizing your web presence so Google, Yahoo!, and other search engines can find you easily. The better you optimize your site using key words and phrases, the higher your brand will appear on search engine results lists when someone searches for your business by name or type.

Remember, a big dog in traditional media or even in the real world may have little or no impact on Facebook. On the social networks, your competition may be a scrappy yet savvy company that has taken the time to build a loyal following. Separate the traditional competition from the Facebook competition, because they may be two different groups for you and your business.

Staying Ahead of the Enemy

Once you find your Facebook competition, observe them. And don't get frustrated if they seem to initially be ahead of the game. Not only is it unrealistic to expect your business to pick up after a few weeks of online marketing, but such quick success can actually be debilitating to a company. Equally unrealistic is believing that you'll always be ahead of the curve, especially if you just started on Facebook.

Making Frienemies

Sometimes our best allies are our adversaries. An old proverb says that "An enemy of my enemy is my friend." That enemy could take several forms, such as a big conglomerate trying to take over your business, or a new start-up inching into your territory.

The situation could call for working with a friendly competitor called, in modern vernacular, a *frienemy*.

DEFINITION

A **frienemy** is a competing person or company that you decide to work with, usually in a limited or carefully defined fashion. Both parties are usually aware that they can switch back to being strictly enemies at any time.

A frienemy relationship can be beneficial to both parties. For instance, let's say you own a chain of tire stores and have a great national TV presence, but Eddie's Tires has an excellent Facebook presence. You could have Eddie promote your stores on Facebook in exchange for you having Eddie do a brief cameo in one of your Fall TV spots. Eddie gets customers via your TV spot, while you get a leg up on your Facebook presence through Eddie's page. And when you both get what you need out of the deal, you can part ways.

The Least You Need to Know

- A social network is a website that lets people connect with like-minded individuals or their favorite brands.
- Your Facebook campaign needs to define, find, and fulfill the customer.
- Prioritize your campaign goals, as they may conflict with one another.
- Make sure your definition of a successful Facebook campaign is quantifiable.
- Working with competitors, called frienemies, can be a great way to get a campaign started.

Your Target Market

Many businesses spin their wheels every year by mass marketing to a geographic area as if everyone living in the area is a potential customer. The reality is that most businesses need a more focused approach: they need to define a target market to sell products and services to.

This is no different with Facebook—not everyone with a Facebook account is a potential customer. In fact, when you consider that Facebook has hundreds of millions of users, you really have to get into the zone and define your target market, or the people who are the most likely to buy from you.

Defining Your Target Market

Within your business, it is important to know the makeup of your customers. The makeup may spell out the age, gender, frequency of purchases, and so on. We recommend creating a spreadsheet listing all of your customers, and then grouping them into different segments that describe their traits. If you utilize a *customer relationship management* (*CRM*) program, this process is much simpler. See Appendix B for some that we recommend.

DEFINITION

Customer relationship management (CRM) is software that enables you to keep track of your customers and prospects to help attract, engage, and maintain relationships.

Everyone who reads this book likely comes from different avenues of life and participates in many different businesses. It doesn't matter if you're a consultant, a marketing manager, or a handyman—you must define who you're marketing to.

Your target market doesn't need to be laser sharp when you're first defining it. For instance, you might start out with a target market of athletic men. Later on, as you get a better sense of your market, you might refine it even more: athletic men in their 30s who live in large metropolitan areas and who love adventure sports.

Knowing your target market helps you define your message so that you can give your audience exactly what they want and need. (We explore more of the application and tools to use for defining your target market in Chapter 5 when we talk about defining the voice of your business and in Chapter 15 when we get into Facebook advertising.)

If you serve a lot of people with a wide variety of characteristics, you might want to consider breaking down your target market into segments, which we discuss in the following section.

Dividing Your Market into Segments

After defining your target market, it's time to break it down into smaller chunks. For example, if your target market is health-care finance professionals—the people in the financial sector of a hospital—you may have products and services for different levels of the organization, from the entry-level billing desk to the CFO of the organization. You might want to divide your target market into the following segments:

- Senior managers who make buying decisions
- Mid-level professionals who manage the products/services you offer
- Entry-level employees who actually use the products/services you offer on a daily basis

Breaking your target market into these smaller categories enables you to fine-tune your messages for the various audiences.

If your target market is senior management, you might approach them with a message that speaks to the strategic attributes of your products and services, possibly providing them with case studies, and short- to long-term results. You might say something like this:

> "Looking to improve your hospital's revenue cycle? Join us for a webinar this week where we cover five case studies from top health-care providers …"

If your target market is mid-level professionals, you might approach them with tactical attributes such as the five steps to improving your daily schedule to increase revenues. Here's a possible marketing pitch:

> "Join us this week to discover the top five steps to improving your hospital's revenue cycle."

If your target market is entry-level employees, you might approach them with attributes that show them how to perform specific job tasks to increase their knowledge and build their skills, such as this:

> "When you talk to patients at the ER desk, you are the first contact in your hospital's revenue cycle. Learn the steps to great customer service."

You can use *segmentation* to divide your market into a variety of categories, including the following:

DEFINITION

Segmentation is the process of dividing people into geographic, demographic, socioeconomic, psychographic, behavioral, and product categories. Segmentation makes it much easier to target your ideal audience.

Geographic segmentation: The intended audience is divided according to geographic units, such as nations, states, regions, counties, cities, or neighborhoods.

Let's say you run a zoo in Brookfield, Illinois. For the most part, you cater to the surrounding areas, but you also pick up some tourists visiting Chicago. Because the zoo caters to people coming to a specific physical location, you should tailor your marketing to people in that geographic area. Facebook makes it possible to focus your posts to only a given country, state, and city (see Figure 2.1). The following steps explain how.

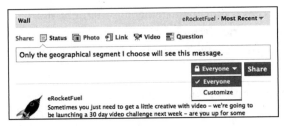

Figure 2.1: *Posting a message on your Fan page to a geographical segment.*

1. Write a post on your Fan page.

2. Click **Everyone** (located below your post).

3. Select **Customize**.

4. Type the name of a country.

5. Depending on the country, Facebook prompts you to further define your desired location.

You also have the option to enter a specific language if that is a desired segment you wish to limit your segmented post to.

Demographic segmentation: The intended audience is divided into categories based on demographic variables (age, income, sex, occupation, education, family size, and the like).

Let's say you work for a national nonprofit organization that wants to get 1,500 college-age kids to volunteer at a benefit concert. You can use Facebook ads to reach a targeted segment of your audience. The Facebook ad platform enables you to segment the exact audience that you want your ads displayed to. So in this example, we are able to pick out men and women between the ages of 17 and 22.

We'll cover Facebook ads in more detail in Chapter 15.

Socioeconomic and psychographic segmentation: In socioeconomic segmentation, the intended audience is divided into a person's work experience and their family's position relative to others, based on income, education, and occupation. With psychographic segmentation, the intended audience is divided according to social class, lifestyle, or personality characteristics.

You can market to each of these segments via Facebook ads based on the details in people's Profiles. You can focus sociological segmentation on a particular group of colleges and workplaces. You can address psychographic segmentation by keywords based on lifestyles.

Behavioral and product-related segmentation: With behavioral segmentation, the intended audience is divided on the basis of their knowledge of, attitude toward, use of, or response to the product. With product-related segmentation, the intended audience for a given product is divided by the amount of product usage, usually categorized demographically or psychographically.

These last types of segmentation present themselves in the course of conversations on Facebook. They are your most active fans—people who are passionate about your brands and are vocal about it. They are almost always heavy users or were once heavy users of your products and services. You won't need to reach out to these people; they will reach out to you.

Harnessing the Power of Social Media

The more Facebook fans you have, the more people you have available to help spread your company's message—and the faster you will grow. This is the key to marketing in social media.

FRIENDLY ADVICE

Hundreds of millions of people log in to Facebook every single day. And the average user has 130 friends. That means that, on average, every Facebook fan puts you in touch with 130 other people. Now that's social marketing!

When you acquire fans on Facebook, you not only have to think about them as individuals but also consider who they know or are connected to.

Imagine if you have 500 fans. If each fan has 130 friends, you have an estimated reach of 65,000 people with the power to further spread your message with a click of a button. It would take most small businesses years to reach that many people using traditional marketing. Facebook has made it possible to reach a huge number of people in a very short time, possibly days. Can you imagine reaching over 65,000 people in a given campaign in one day? What would that do for your business in terms of buzz, exposure, and potential sales?

Now, you probably won't reach 100 percent of these people in your marketing efforts. But there's a good chance a large percentage of these people will at least glimpse your brand as they interact with their friends on Facebook. At the onset of marketing, it's all about exposure to your brand. As people see your brand, they'll start to form an idea that your company is one that has already influenced one of their friends and already have a positive attitude toward it.

Have you ever heard of the term "six degrees of separation"? It's the idea that, on average, everyone is only six steps away from a relationship with anyone else on the planet. Facebook makes it easy for people to see each other's connections; it's up to you to take advantage of them.

Last year, John's agency eRocketFuel ran a series of Facebook ads targeting dry cleaners after John spoke at a national conference for cleaners. His ads and posts on the DryCleaning and Laundry Institute (DLI) Facebook page were seen by many cleaners. This led to many friend requests and fans on the eRocketFuel Fan page.

That, in turn, led to articles published in *Crain's*, a national business magazine, and more than 15 speaking engagements with dry cleaners from New York City to Raleigh, North Carolina, all the way to Australia. It also led to consulting contracts with several dry cleaners all around the world—all by harnessing a little segmentation on Facebook.

Marketing to Individual Segments

Demographic, psychographic, and geographic attributes help you to connect to people in a way that speaks directly to them. A person's demographic and psychographic makeup may contribute to the way she interacts on Facebook and her many preferences.

For example, Generation Y college students tend to have the following key attributes that you might want to consider before marketing to them:

- They are resistant to advertising and being sold to.
- They are socially conscious about a better world.
- They are anti-corporate.
- They speak their mind and dress as they please.
- They are individualistic and idealistic.

These characteristics help explain why social media is so popular with this demographic. With social media, the students are in control of whom they interact with, and they can voice their opinions. Now, as a business trying to reach such a young segment, you have to do more than just be present on Facebook. You need to talk to them appropriately, which we discuss in Chapter 5.

FEEDBACK

Don't make the mistake of thinking that teens are the only demographic on Facebook. The fastest-growing segment using Facebook and other social media are people age 55 and older. Watch out, little whippersnappers.

What about geography? It makes sense that people relate well to things that happen in their neighborhoods, hometowns, and even states. That's when they stop and really take notice.

If a catastrophe takes place 5 miles from you, wouldn't you stop and listen longer than if the same thing happened halfway around the globe? The same goes for marketing on Facebook: keeping your focus on the geographic segments that matter most to you will generate the biggest impact.

Is your business participating in a local charity run? How about a coat drive for children? Are you going to be at a festival this weekend? Let your fans know about it. These are the things that make people smile and interact with your business.

Creating Niches

To market effectively to the various segments within your target, consider placing them into *niches*. Niches are different than segments on Facebook in that they allow you to dive further into specific attributes.

Breaking your customers down even further enables you to create marketing messages and conversations tailored to each niche. Dividing your segments into niches may seem tedious now, but it will pay off.

DEFINITION

Niches are subsets of a target market segment.

The health-care finance example from earlier in this chapter identified three market segments: CFOs, mid-level professionals, and entry-level employees. Because all of their needs are so different, you might want to set up different Facebook pages for each of them. If you present your information to all of them on a single page, a lot of that information won't apply to a big chunk of your audience, and you will begin to lose fans. You have to remain focused to retain fans. You can use the status tool to customize who the message appears to, but if your messages are regularly posted and segmented for large amounts of people, this can be very tedious.

Defining Niches on Facebook

It's easy to say that everyone in the world is a potential customer, but you already know that such a scattershot approach isn't the most effective way to market yourself on Facebook. Instead, think about a commonality among your potential customers that you can use to define a niche.

For example, suppose you run a web design business. Looking back at your projects for the past year, you see that most of your customers for the last month have been stay-at-home moms. Another commonality is that all of the websites you designed in December were for restaurants. And yet another commonality is that 80 percent of your business is with nonprofits. You've just identified three prime niches: stay-at-home moms, restaurants, and nonprofits.

Depending on the size of these niches and how much business they can bring in, you just might want to consider creating three separate Facebook Groups that focus on these areas and invite individuals in these niches to join these groups. (For details on creating Facebook Group pages, see Chapter 8.)

WATCH OUT

Be careful not to group too many people with different interests into one area on Facebook. It dilutes the effectiveness of the conversation.

To Niche or Not to Niche

If you have a smaller audience of a hundred people, you may not need to niche at all, at least at first. But as you grow your Facebook presence, you may find that the topics you discuss aren't engaging large percentages of the fans who frequent your page. If this goes on for too long, people will leave. You want to start creating niches before you lose your audience.

After you define your niches, you need to fill them with the appropriate customers to make loyal fans. Facebook provides many ways to fill your niches with the appropriate people, including the following:

- Discussing the topics that matter to the niche

- Building niche pages or groups (see Chapters 7 and 8)

- Running targeted ads (see Chapter 15)

- Conducting questions (see Chapter 3)

- Using the Facebook search tool (see next section)

Searching for People on Facebook

If you know the names of people you want to include in your niche, you can search for them on Facebook and message them. To search for people by name, type the name in the Search box that appears at the top of every Facebook page (see Figure 2.2). If there are multiple users with the same name, a list appears identifying users by their city and state. If you don't see the person you're looking for on that list, click **See More Results** at the bottom of the page.

Figure 2.2: *Search for people by simply typing in their names.*

When you find the person you're looking for, you can send him a message by clicking the **Message** button at the top right of the page to invite him to your Facebook page or simply communicate with him (see Figure 2.3).

Message

Figure 2.3: *Click the* **Message** *button to send a note.*

WATCH OUT

Be careful about contacting too many people you don't know using the Facebook Message tool. Facebook frowns on this method because spammers use this tactic to find, friend, and fan people they don't know. If you do this too often, Facebook will ban you from using the Message tool or requesting friends for a certain period of time.

Marketing to Them Strategically

Here's the trick with marketing on Facebook as well as all other social media platforms: do so sparingly and with as much transparency as possible. That's not to say that you can't ever post a message saying, "Check out our latest products," but you should use these types of messages sparingly as a last resort, and only after you've started developing relationships with people.

FEEDBACK

Marketing transparency is when a business gives customers an incentive to buy without actually having to use the word "sell." The business is offering something so useful to the customer that it doesn't have to do the hard sell. Often what the business offers includes free goods or services in exchange for a bigger commitment.

Transparency is talking about the topic of a product or service with the intent to educate without saying "buy now." Consider how you react when you read a great article or blog describing a product or service versus looking at an advertisement. Most people prefer being informed of products of services through the blog or article rather than through an ad, and this approach is the best way to market on Facebook.

People join your Fan page because they're interested in your brand and how your brand addresses other topics that appeal to them. When you bombard them with a lot of ads or overt sales pitches, they feel like you're selling a used car to them.

People like to buy things, but they don't like to be "sold to" in the traditional sense. So use some tact in your marketing approach, and never say, "Oh boy, do I have a deal for you. But wait, that's not all ...."

Here's what you should do to market your products or services:

- Share relevant information from your website.

- Educate them on the product topics, but don't overtly sell to them.

- Share fun things like recipes, music videos, and photos of children (try to keep it relevant to your brand as much as you can).

- Use videos and images to enhance your content.

Mimicking Their Voice

When you think about your audience, do certain adjectives come to mind? Do you think of them as forward-thinking, passionate, technology hungry, total geeks? Or maybe you'd describe them as old school, aloof, and quiet?

People in the same niche generally talk similarly. In order to connect with them, you need to replicate their voice in your communications.

Consider a business that caters to engineers. Engineers are very precise individuals who generally use very logical language. If you were to use a lot of slang in a very casual tone, you might turn them off. Instead, engineers might prefer a more direct, professional approach—one that follows a logical progression and that lays out what the problem, potential solutions, and potential challenges are, as well as all the resources available to solve the problem.

If your audience is a group of new moms, you might address them in this manner:

- Use smart, calming language that focuses on the well-being and education of their children.

- Share research or stories from other moms on why they should not serve certain foods to their children. The key point here is that you're using their voice to drive content.

- Ask your fans to review toys, cribs, strollers, and even mom-care products like breast pumps and food mills.

- Use video to show—not just tell—moms how to soothe a crying baby with swaddling techniques and sounds.

We explore voice in detail in Chapter 5.

Let's say you have a tattoo shop, skateboard park, or bar. Your marketing approach should be different for each. It's possible that the audience of a tattoo shop will love it if you are too brash and rude on Facebook. If that's their thing, go for it. Use the approach that reaches your audience. Just be careful how far you take this voice in your marketing messaging. It may be the audience's voice, but the best way to cater to them might be to provide a forum for them to interact in but not to actually mirror their voice yourself.

Generating a Positive Response

The techniques for generating a positive response from your audience depend on the audience and their preferences. Choose a path based upon your knowledge of your audience, and test it out. If the audience likes it, keep it up. If they don't like it, try something else.

Here are some ideas to start with to get some positive energy on your Facebook pages:

- Share success stories and ask fans what they think.

- Ask fans to share their success stories.

- Ask fans what their favorite parts about your products/services are and assure them that their responses will help you make them better.

- Praise them for being the best fans ever.

- Occasionally give away prizes to fans.

- Highlight a fan of the month based on how much he or she interacted with your site.

Think about what sorts of things elicit positive and negative reactions as you go about your day. These same things will probably elicit similar responses from your fans on Facebook.

Identifying Their Needs and Wants

Facebook is a great place to conduct market research for your business. You can use it to come up with ideas for new products/services, or to revamp existing products/ services.

For example, if you run a business that sells imported olive oils and balsamic vinegars, and you want to start selling new flavors, you can ask your fans for their opinions. You can do this by using the free Question tool on your Wall.

Here's what you do:

1. On your Fan page, click **Question** (see Figure 2.4).

2. Type your question in the box that appears.

3. Add as many answers as you like.

4. If you want to enable fans to add their own answers to the list of answers you provide, click **Allow anyone to add options**.

5. Click **Ask Question**.

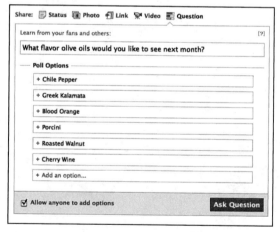

Figure 2.4: *A question on Facebook.*

The Least You Need to Know

- Take the time to define who you are marketing to.
- Divide your target market into different market segments for easier communication.
- Avoid grouping too many people with different interests into one area on Facebook.
- Market on Facebook with as much transparency as possible.
- When communicating, pay attention to how people in a specific segment and niche talk, and then mimic that way of communicating when you interact with them as appropriate.

Your Facebook Marketing Plan

In This Chapter

- Building a solid marketing plan
- Understanding the importance of defining your products and services
- Deciding on your promotional approach for fans
- Setting up an effective marketing calendar
- Writing strategic Facebook content

Your business needs to have a Facebook marketing plan that lays out the path to take to achieve your goals in a given timeline. By putting your plan in writing, you're far more likely to hit your targets in a timely fashion.

Facebook is in many ways a very spontaneous marketing tool, because personal users tend to focus on the present moment when using Facebook. For this reason, many businesses don't feel that they need a social media marketing plan. But just like in traditional marketing, you need a Facebook marketing plan that focuses on who the target market is, how they can be reached, and what the best tools are to do so.

When you're using Facebook as a marketing tool, you have to be strategic, but you also need to be flexible enough to adjust when your marketing results call for it.

Dare to be different from most businesses that use Facebook to market their products and services. Treat your Facebook marketing plan as an actual business tool. In our experience, the businesses that give Facebook the marketing attention it deserves always get a return on their investment of time, money, and resources.

Developing a Marketing Program

As you read the next few sections, start jotting down answers to the questions we ask, and use these answers to begin crafting your own social media marketing plan. Also start writing down your Facebook goals, promotional content, and design ideas. Use these notes to develop a full-blown marketing plan.

Mapping Out Your Goals

So what are your Facebook marketing goals? Here are some examples of goals for various types of businesses:

- A business owner or president might want to make more money.

- A marketing director might want to get more brand exposure.

- A nonprofit organization might want to increase the number of volunteers and get more donations.

- An association might want to use Facebook as a networking medium for their members.

All of these are legitimate goals, and you can use Facebook to achieve them. Think of Facebook as a means to an end. It's not just a marketing tool for promoting your brand, but a window into the wants and needs of your audience.

To begin the process of developing your Facebook marketing plan, list your immediate goals, your goals for three months from now, and your goals for a year from now. Here's a sample list to get you thinking in the right direction:

- **Immediate goals:** Set up a Facebook page, launch it, and invite everyone on your email list to join you.

- **Three-month goals:** Acquire 250 fans, have your posts prewritten for the following month's marketing, and launch your first advertising campaign.

- **One-year goal:** Have 500+ active fans who provide you with feedback on the research questions you ask each month.

Other common Facebook goals for businesses include the following:

- Generating more brand exposure
- Driving traffic to your website
- Providing customer service
- Identifying new customers
- Retaining existing customers
- Performing market research
- Selling products and services on Facebook
- Using Facebook as a communications tool

FEEDBACK

Map out your goals before proceeding with this book. When you have completed them, prioritize them and make sure they are measurable, realistic, and can be accomplished within a specific timeline.

Choosing Which Products and Services to Feature

Identify what products and services you want to promote on Facebook. Define these products or services and identify their key attributes and benefits. If you sell hundreds of products or services, select a few of them to focus on at any given time. Think of Facebook as a homepage of a website. In effect, it's a portal into your larger offerings. If you have too much going on up front, you're going to confuse your users, and they might leave. Instead, feature no more than 10 products or services. In fact, the fewer products or services you feature, the better, as your page will be clearer and easier to use. If you only have one or two products or services, that's to your advantage when marketing on Facebook.

The following figures show how businesses are using Facebook to display a limited number of products and services. Review these to see which model fits your business.

The Geneva Cleaners Facebook Fan page (see Figure 3.1) features a simple call to action. All the customer has to do is sign up for the business's email club.

Welcome to Geneva Cleaners

Geneva Cleaners has been providing dry cleaning services to Geneva and the surrounding communities, including Batavia and St. Charles, Illinois for over 50 years. We offer a variety of services and have a company-wide commitment of reducing our environmental footprint. We do this by using low-impact cleaning products, state of the art cleaning machines and reducing excessive paper and plastic waste with our increasingly popular "Green Bags."

We are a full-service dry cleaner and offer a variety of services including:
- Car Hop Drive-up Service
- Express Bag Service
- Same Day Service
- Executive Shirt Service
- Household Fabrics
- Draperies
- Pillow Service
- Decorative Pillows
- Comforters, Blankets, and Quilts
- Leathers, Suedes, and Furs
- Wedding Gown Cleaning, Preservation and Heirloom
- Alterations & Tailoring
- Fire Restoration Services

Join Our Email Club!

* Required Fields

* First Name:

* Last Name:

* Phone Number:

* Email Address:

(Join Now!)

Figure 3.1: *The Geneva Cleaners Fan page on Facebook.*

The National Wildlife Federation (NWF; see Figure 3.2) keeps it simple by dividing its Fan page into three sections. Two of the sections link to the website, where fans can learn more about the organization or purchase a product. The third option encourages users to share the Fan page with their friends. The page is simple, inspiring, and to the point.

Figure 3.2: *The National Wildlife Federation Fan page on Facebook.*

Similarly, the American Association of Medical Assistants (AAMA) Fan page is divided into seven sections (see Figure 3.3).

Figure 3.3: *The American Association of Medical Assistants Fan page on Facebook.*

The fewer areas and actions you feature on your Fan page, the easier it will be for your audience to use. AAMA and the NWF are businesses with a lot of products, yet they concentrate on just a few areas of their business to make the display more manageable for Facebook users. The Geneva Cleaners Fan page is even simpler. The business wants you to Like its page and fill out a form to receive more information. Smaller service-based businesses should take Geneva Cleaners' lead when developing their Facebook page.

By keeping your Fan page simple, you're making it easier to market your business on Facebook. If you sell more than 10 products or services, feature the additional products or services on your business website, not on Facebook.

Choosing Your Promotion Strategies

For any business to grow, it needs to make itself known to more people. To generate awareness, you need to run promotions. Facebook offers several promotional tools for getting your marketing message out to your current fans, friends of your fans, and people who fit the description of your target market.

Facebook offers the following promotional opportunities:

- **Facebook ads:** You can purchase ads that appear in the right-hand column of pages throughout Facebook. They are delivered to targeted audiences based on users' Profiles. A Facebook ad can include an image and text, and it's sometimes paired with news about social actions (such as Liking a page) that a user's friends may have taken. Chapter 15 explores ads in detail.

- **Sponsored stories:** These are a type of Facebook ad where your friends' and fans' activities are turned into promotions. These fee-based stories also show up on the right column of pages on Facebook. They are more subtle than ads and potentially have greater impact. Find out more about Sponsored Stories in Chapter 15.

- **Contests, sweepstakes, trivia, and coupons:** Facebook doesn't have apps for these features, but you can use third-party apps to run these sorts of promotions. See Chapter 10 for details on contests.

- **Facebook Deals:** Deals are based on people's Facebook check-ins when they visit your business. You can run check-in deals across multiple store locations and create different types of deals to achieve different business objectives. Find out more about deals in Chapter 18.

- **Facebook Marketplace:** The Marketplace is a Facebook site dedicated to selling personal goods and services; it's similar to a classified ad site, where you can find cars, rentals, real estate, and even fish tanks. Turn to Chapter 17 for more details about the Facebook Marketplace.

FRIENDLY ADVICE

Vary your promotions each month to get the most out of your Facebook marketing campaign. Facebook ads and contests are very effective in growing a large fan base.

All of these promotional options offer great opportunities to get more exposure to your fans. In strategizing which ones make sense for your company, refer back to your goals. The following table lists various goals and the best promotional tool for achieving that goal.

Choosing the Right Promotional Tool for Your Goals

Goal	Promotional Tool
Drive targeted traffic to your Fan page	Facebook ads
Drive targeted traffic to your Fan page from the friends of the people who are already fans	Sponsored stories
Drive traffic to your Fan page and get people to tell their friends about your page	Contests, sweepstakes, trivia, and coupons
Drive on-foot traffic to your retail location	Facebook Deals
Sell personal items	Facebook Marketplace

Users get tired of seeing the same promotions. Mix them up so that you're not always doing the same thing over and over. In Chapter 4, we talk about how to use these promotional strategies to maximize them in your marketing campaigns.

Creating a Marketing Calendar

Your marketing calendar serves as your road map to your complete Facebook marketing schedule for the next year. Keeping a close eye on your calendar helps keep your campaigns on schedule.

The most efficient way to build your calendar is to use a program that can store the actual messages you plan to post on Facebook. A spreadsheet is one way to accomplish this.

Here are some types of information you should include on the calendar as Facebook posts:

- **Sales and promotions of your products and service.** This can be a 10 percent sale on all blue shirts, or $7 ties for anyone whose name is John. Get creative. Plan your online sales to complement your offline sales.

- **Lighthearted posts to elicit humor.** Use jokes and funny pictures to get a response from your fans. Your posts don't always have to be about the business. Consider posting a picture of a dog or a baby doing something funny. Schedule these as the need arises to break up the monotony—once a week is a good idea.

- **Contests.** Contests are a surefire way to drive traffic to your site and build your fan base. Schedule these on a monthly basis.

FRIENDLY ADVICE

Be sure to clearly indicate on your marketing calendar when promotions start and end. Additionally, be adamant about tracking as many data points as possible so you know what is working and what is not. This will help you to refine your marketing plan in the future for things that are not working well.

- **Other creative items such as video, live appearances, and so on.** Think of your marketing calendar as your main resource for all the things you're going to do to sell your products/services on Facebook. Anything that comes up, make sure to slot it into the calendar.

Scheduling Posts

When scheduling the frequency of your posts, it's best to limit them to no more than three times per week. If every post generates a big fan response, you can gradually increase the frequency. Additionally, don't post more than one sales promotion per week. Any more than this and you'll come off as being very sales-oriented and you may lose fans.

People are most active on Facebook on Thursday, Friday, and Saturday, so these are the best days for promotions. We talk more about your content strategy and other days and times to post in Chapter 5.

Figure 3.4 shows postings on a marketing calendar from a dry cleaner. Notice that the business has scheduled up to three postings a week, mixing questions with promotional messages and jokes.

Date	Content	Link
30-Jul	All that Glitters and Shines! Did you know that not all sequins and beads can withstand drycleaning? Bring your favorite sequined item to Geneva Cleaners and we will test your garment to make sure it will endure cleaning.	http://www.example.com
25-Jul	What is your favorite Geneva store? Other than Geneva Cleaners (of course) **wink wink**	http://www.example.com
23-Jul	Don't forget... Due to the heat we are only offering same day service until 10am this week! Stay cool Chicagoland!	http://www.example.com
20-Jul	Beat the Heat! Save 2 trips to the dry cleaner with our FREE Home Delivery/Pickup service - you can sign up online!	http://www.example.com
18-Jul	TGIF Facebook fans! What are your plans for this awesome August weekend?	http://www.example.com
16-Jul	Green your life! Get your reusable Green Garmento bag at Geneva Cleaners. Be fantastic...Use less plastic!	http://www.example.com
14-Jul	Did you know this is Simplify Your Life week? Let us take care of life's messy stains and help you simplify your life.	http://www.example.com
12-Jul	Happy National Ice Cream Month from Geneva Cleaners! What's your favorite scoop?	http://www.example.com
9-Jul	As we celebrate the final Harry Potter movie let's look back at the series from the past decade! Who is going to the midnight showing?	http://www.example.com
6-Jul	Have you ever had a question or two for the drycleaner? Or even wondered what in the world is drycleaning? Join our email club to get the insides of the cleaning world as well as the latest happenings at Geneva Cleaners!	http://www.example.com
4-Jul	Have you Got Milk? (tm)... How about milk clothes???	http://www.example.com

Figure 3.4: A sample marketing calendar.

If you sell a line of pies to quick-service restaurants, school programs, and bakeries, you probably already have a marketing plan for selling those pies. In your marketing plan, you probably send out emails, postcards, and sales sheets; go to tradeshows; and make calls on a weekly basis.

Here's a sample marketing schedule for promoting three different kinds of pies:

Product	Email #1	Email #2	Postcard	Facebook #1
Apple Pies	Jan 1	Jan 15	Jan 5	Jan 2
Guava Pies	Jan 1	Jan 15	Jan 5	Jan 11
Cherry Pies	Jan 1	Jan 15	Jan 5	Jan 19

Notice how you promote all pies via email on the first and fifteenth of the month. And you promote all of them again using a postcard on the fifth. You can use Facebook promotions to fill in the gaps in the marketing calendar. And because Facebook is so easy to use and many promotion strategies are free, you can promote individual products rather than bulking them together.

Deviating from Your Schedule

If possible, format your marketing calendar so that it shows your Facebook promotions on a weekly basis. Keep in mind, however, that not every action you take on Facebook will appear on your calendar. For instance, you might not schedule a Facebook post for Monday, but if on Monday a fan replies to one of your posts, or she starts a post, you need to reply to it promptly. Facebook users expect speedy responses to their posts.

Make time in your schedule to check your Facebook page for posts and to reply back as needed. It's a good practice to do this three times a day. This process doesn't need to eat up a lot of your time. We recommend that you give yourself 15 minutes several times a day to review and reply to posts.

Additionally, always leave a spot open each week for breaking news. It's okay for these kinds of in-the-moment posts to trump your scheduled posts because most of the time they bring even more attention to your page than any promotion could. It's the nature of people to want to know something important that just happened.

Here are a few breaking-news examples:

- The softball team your business sponsors wins their league championship
- One of your employees receives a community-service award from a local charity
- A local citizen decides to run for state office
- Your local high school football team hosts a home game against a major rival
- A terrible storm is heading for your area
- The Chicago Cubs win the World Series

Each of these may grab the attention of your fans and ignite some hot conversation. Is this off the topic of your business? Sure. But it's part of building relationships on Facebook. Get to know your fans.

Similarly, you need to be willing to jump outside of the plan you created when special circumstances introduce themselves. For example, if a tornado just hit a small city in your part of the country and ravaged all of the buildings and homes, you should be willing to adjust your marketing schedule to mention the event.

A business might post the following after a disaster hits:

- Our hearts go out to the many lives that were lost.

- Want to help with the recovery? Go to www.redcross.org.

- In times of difficulty, our humanity compels us to help one another.

Deciding on Topics

When it comes to deciding on what topics to post about on Facebook, separate your topics into several categories:

- Informational and educational content

- Questions and polls

- Promotions

- Lighthearted topics, jokes, and other humor

Mix this up to fit the scope of your business. Post your content at the same time each week. Having a formula makes it easy for you and your team to generate posts, and your fans know what to expect. People like predictability. It's what keeps them grounded and organized.

Figuring How Much Time to Spend on Marketing

Most businesses spend about four hours a week or less managing their social media presence. We encourage you to schedule a minimum of four hours into your weekly plan, but you should plan to spend more time on your Facebook marketing campaign when you're first getting it up and running. As you grow and start to do more business online, the required amount of time in a given week will also increase.

Think of Facebook as another marketing format—along with newsletters; radio, TV, and print advertising; conferences; and anything else you to do to promote your business—and give it the same amount of energy you give to these other marketing efforts.

Crafting Your Posts

Writing posts on Facebook is part art and part science. Every audience is unique and has a particular way that they like to communicate. A local country band may end every post with "We love ya'll more than mama's apple pie." It's colloquial, it's local, and it's just plain fun. At the same time, your posts need to be predictable and elicit a reaction from your fans.

You need to tailor the style of your posts to your business and your audience. If you interact with the general public, and you have a business where humor is acceptable—such as a barber shop or ice cream shop—make your posts funny. If your business is a little more professional or conservative, such as an accounting firm or a chiropractor office, stick to delivering data and facts. You know your customers better than anyone, so make sure to deliver them the content that they want.

Your messages should reflect what your customers want to hear—not just what you want to share. Here are some ideas:

- Breaking news

- White papers on the latest research

- Pictures of new products

- How-to video demonstrations

- Jokes and other humorous posts (Refer to Figure 3.5 to see how a dry cleaner used humor to attract more Facebook fans.)

FRIENDLY ADVICE

Even the stuffiest business people like a little humor now and then, so be sure to mix up your messages to keep your users entertained.

Figure 3.5: *The Geneva Cleaners dog Facebook ad.*

Facebook is a space where people network and communicate primarily with their friends. As a business, you're in a more secondary role. To blend in and not appear too pushy, you need to act more casual than you would on a strictly business forum. If your fans wanted you to be completely professional, they'd be on a different social network, such as *LinkedIn*.

> **DEFINITION**
>
> **LinkedIn** is the largest professional social networking website, with over 120 million users from around the world. The focus on LinkedIn is to network to find jobs, partners, and clients.

Developing Content

When deciding what to say, start with what you know and what you can share that's valuable to potential fans and current customers. People love to hear about the latest and greatest features on products that they use. Start by writing a few posts that direct users to your website or blog.

For instance, if you run a deli, you might steer readers to your web page, where you provide nutritional data for all of your sandwiches and soups. If you're a law firm, you might post a weekly legal tip. If you're a handyman, you might feature a brief how-to video for various simple household fixes, such as tightening a leaky faucet. Another idea for a handyman is to include seasonal tips, such as "It's that time of year again: have you cleaned the leaves and debris from your rain gutters?"

You can even push your fans to other resources. These may be products or services that you don't offer but are still a great value. The handyman may post a link to a hardware store that shows a picture of the kinds of doors that are available to purchase. A landscaper could post a link to some famous lawns and lawn ornaments of movie stars. And a dentist might post a link to a video that explains how tooth decay forms on a tooth when it's not properly cared for.

> **FRIENDLY ADVICE**
>
> Why would you ever want to push your fans to websites other than your own? Because doing so signals to your fans that you care about what's best for your clients and customers. Such actions build trust, signaling to users that they can depend on you as a resource and that you're not solely interested in selling your products and services. If you have something to offer, by all means, share it. If not, let users know about others who might be able to help them. Think about it this way: if it's something you'd do for a friend, why not do it for a fan?

On a weekly or monthly basis, you should set aside some time to brainstorm original content ideas for the month. We recommend gathering your team in a creative setting (outside the office works best) and detaching yourself from cell phones, computers, and even Facebook. Your goal should be to generate original ideas, not to copy others.

Asking Your Audience What They Want to Hear

If you're struggling to come up with ideas, consider asking your audience for suggestions. Ask your fans what they want to hear about by using the Question tool. You can even use the poll options to set up a question so that it can have multiple answers.

For example, if you run a printing company, your question might look like this:

We're planning our editorial calendar for the next six months and would like your input on the topics we cover in our upcoming posts. So far we are planning to cover the following topics:

- *Building a better business card*

- *Turning thank-you notes into up-sell opportunities*

- *Using postcards in marketing campaigns*

Please provide three suggestions for topics you'd like to learn about:

- _____

- _____

- _____

By approaching content in this way, your audience is part of the team that creates. And they love the idea that you are asking them for this.

Keeping It Short and Sweet

People generally don't actually read content on the web like they read books. Instead, they skim. This goes for Facebook, too. That means that they typically only see keywords that are meaningful to them, and they skip the rest. This is why it's important to keep your posts short and to the point.

Facebook enables you to post up to 420 characters. If you go over this limit, Facebook won't allow you to post your message. If you have a longer post, you may use the Facebook Note feature. While notes are great for longer posts, they aren't as effective in terms of visibility. Use them sparingly. You can read more about notes in Chapter 7.

Can you imagine if a business page you Liked posted multiple, lengthy messages to its Facebook site every day? It wouldn't take long for you to either Unlike the business or hide the page.

The Least You Need to Know

- Write down a list of immediate, three-month, and one-year goals.
- Plan to spend at least four hours a week managing your social media presence.
- If you interact with the general public, and you have a business where humor is acceptable, make your posts funny.
- Be willing to adjust your marketing plan to account for major current events and other breaking news.

Facebook Campaigns

In This Chapter

- Learning how to set up a Facebook campaign
- Establishing goals
- Thinking outside the box
- Measuring your results

Now that you've defined your Facebook strategy and built your marketing plan, it's time to roll up your sleeves and start a Facebook campaign. This chapter shows you how to harness Facebook's many components to run a successful marketing campaign.

The Components

When running a *Facebook campaign*, you can draw on several Facebook components. These include:

- Wall posts
- Unique page tabs
- Facebook ads
- Sponsored stories
- Email marketing

DEFINITION

A **Facebook campaign** is a systematic course of aggressive activities used to attain more Likes for your Fan page. These Likes translate into customers and clients.

The following sections explore how to use each of these Facebook components in your campaigns.

Wall Posts

One major benefit of Wall posts is that they encourage your fans to engage with you by taking an action, whether that action is simply to read or glance at your post, click a link, or even share your posts with friends.

Except for the glance, each of these actions is measureable. You can track how many times a Wall post was viewed, commented on, the percentage of feedback, and how it compared to other posts in the previous 30 days of posts. You can use these metrics to help you to figure out what Wall posts your fans respond to favorably and which ones are a waste of your time. The metrics also help you Facebook post writing skills. (For details on interaction and tracking methods, see Chapter 16.)

You should update your posts on at least a weekly basis, but keep in mind that it may take several campaigns to get people to start responding to your Facebook posts. Be conversational, authentic, and personal by sharing videos and photos of your business. Your local community and customers will value these personal posts because they can relate to them.

Additionally, the more time you put into developing creative posts that ask your fans for their opinion, the more engagement you will get out of your fans. For instance, ask people what they think about your products and how can they be improved. Questions are your magic messaging format for Wall posts (see Figure 4.1).

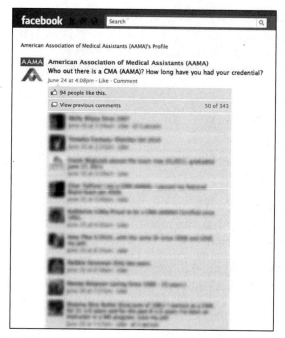

Figure 4.1: *Wall posts that use multiple questions generally get better response rates.*

A secondary use of Wall posts is to post on other people's or companies' Walls on behalf of your company. This can be tricky but, if done right, can harness a lot of fans.

Don't post blatant marketing messages on other people's Walls. For example, writing something like, "Come check out the great deals we have at XYZ Fan page" is a serious no-no. The owner of the Fan page may flag your post as spam, which will result in a mark on your account, and Facebook could freeze your account.

A better approach would be to offer assistance in some way. Here's an example of how this might play out with two local businesses, one a local dry cleaner called Phil's and the other a county baseball park that's home of the Cougars baseball team.

The dry cleaner's goal is to build up their fan base to over 1,000 fans. They survey the local businesses' Facebook Fan pages and notice that the county baseball park has more than 5,000 fans. They decide to go to the baseball Fan page logged in as the dry cleaner page, Like the page, and then post a message.

They post, "Great game last night—our staff at Phil's Dry Cleaning was at your stadium celebrating our summer party. Let me know if I can help push some of our fans to your page. We're in this town together. Go Cougars!"

Unique Page Tabs

A tab is a link that you can place in the left column of your Fan page under your Facebook Profile to direct people to your various Facebook pages. By default, many Fan pages have tabs for their Wall, Info, Friend Activity, Photos, and Discussion Board.

For your campaign, consider pushing people to a custom Facebook page that gets them to take an action. One action might be to join a contest and, in the process, give you their contact information.

These custom tabs (see Figure 4.2) encourage fans to explore what you have to offer while on Facebook. You can embed any number of elements in your tabs, including the following:

- Contests
- Videos
- Free downloads
- Case studies
- Maps
- Tweets
- Blog posts
- Sign-up forms
- Online stores

Figure 4.2: *Audi's Fan page highlights four custom tabs: 2011 Le Mans Victory, Welcome, A7 Bold Design, and Audi quattro.*

Facebook Ads

Facebook ads are incredible tools to get people to Like your page (see Figure 4.3). Facebook displays ads based on a user's Profile information—the information Facebook users fill out when they set up their account, including age, sex, location, favorite music, sport teams, books, and so on.

> **DEFINITION**
>
> A **Facebook ad** is an online advertisement. The ads are targeted to Facebook user demographics per the request of the person buying an ad. They show up on the right column of every user's account.

Because ads display based on user demographic information, a Facebook user who is a college-educated 37-year-old male living in Chicago would see an entirely different set of ads than a 79-year-old woman who lives on a farm in rural Nebraska and has never gone to college. In Chapter 3, we talk about the importance of defining who your target market is, what they do, where they live, and their ages. This is where such data really come into play. You use this data when developing your Facebook ad campaign (see Chapter 15).

FEEDBACK

One of the cool Facebook ad features that can add fuel to your campaign is to pick the option to advertise to friends of current fans. The friends will see a message next to the ad saying that their friend Likes your page. This is social proof for your Fan page and encourages them to Like it as well.

Figure 4.3: *Three different Facebook ads that are custom to author John Wayne Zimmerman based on his demographic information and other information he put in his Profile.*

Sponsored Stories

Sponsored stories are a form of a Facebook ad in which you transform your friends' and fans' activities, such as posts and Likes, into promotions (see Figure 4.4).

These are one of the most under-utilized campaign tools on the Facebook platform, but don't let that deter you. Used strategically as testimonials, they can be very effective.

We recommend that you use some of your best posts and those of your fans to run as Sponsored Stories. Your best posts are the ones that have spurred your fans to take action, either by responding to your post, purchasing a product or service, or sharing the post.

You can repurpose fans' best posts as testimonials. For example, suppose you're putting on an event and are trying to get 1,000 people to attend. Twelve hours before the event begins, 750 people are registered. This is the perfect time to post the following message on your Wall:

> "Just hit 750 registrants for the 'Who's your daddy of Facebook Marketing' webinar. Will we hit 1,000?"

If someone posts the following reply on your Wall:

> "Looking forward to your awesome webinar today. I just registered."

You could post this as a second sponsored story (see Figure 4.4 for a great example of this). The power behind such an ad is that it's a living, breathing testimonial that someone wants to attend your event. It also provides a live update with a deadline that pushes people to react.

Figure 4.4: *Taking posts from your Wall and making them work for you as a sponsored story.*

Email Marketing

Email marketing remains one of the biggest internet marketing tools today. When coupled with other Facebook marketing tools, email can be a killer marketing strategy. As you begin to build up your Facebook presence, you should use email to send your customers Facebook invitations that showcase valuable content or promote a product or service.

Promotional emails that push people to your page for a special are a great way to get your audience to visit your Facebook page. We call this kind of marketing *push marketing*. While they are there, make sure to ask for their information—we call this kind of marketing *pull marketing*.

> **DEFINITION**
>
> **Push marketing** is any kind of marketing that gets users to go somewhere, like a website or Fan page, for information or a special.
>
> **Pull marketing** is the process of the individual user giving you information—for instance, inviting users to provide you with their email address in order to receive a newsletter.

Sending promotional emails every other week is a great way to keep your communication channel open to your customers. And when you push them to your Facebook page with emails, they can respond to you and other customers who may have the same wants/needs/concerns.

An example of an email promotion that utilizes a push and a pull to a Facebook page may look like this:

> "Next Year's Annual conference will either be in Las Vegas or Orlando. We'd love to know where you think it should be. Share your opinions on our Facebook page. Click the link below to let us know. Thank you."

Establishing Your Campaign Goals

To maximize the various Facebook components we just described, you should first determine the goals of your specific campaign. Answer the following questions to help establish your goals:

- Do you want to simply create Facebook fans and get as many Likes as possible?

  If so, give Facebook advertising a go (see Chapter 15).

- Do you want to push people back to your website where you can introduce them to multiple products and services?

  If so, use a combination of all of the components.

- Do you already have a large email list and you want to convert that list to Likes?

  If so, use the Invite tool within Facebook to invite people to join your Fan page or email them the link to your Facebook page.

- Are you trying to get people to register for a webinar?

  If so, use email, Sponsored Stories, and Facebook ads.

- Do you want to conduct a survey to determine the needs and wants of your existing fan base?

  If so, use third-party programs for surveys (see Appendix B), or the Question sharing tool on your Fan page Wall.

- Are you trying to find new customers for your products and services?

  If so, all of the components will help you to accomplish this.

Each campaign you launch should have its own unique goal. For instance, if you have a subscription-based magazine website that offers the latest tips and tricks for web designers, you might select one of the following goals for your campaign:

- Increase subscriptions

- Sell branded products such as hats, t-shirts, stickers, etc.

- Get members to share the website link with their friends

- Increase views of videos

- Increase Facebook fans

Try not to create a campaign with multiple goals. Keeping the goal simple makes it easier to track what does and doesn't work.

Composing Your Campaign Message

The campaign message you send should be clear and to the point. People want to see what it is you're promoting without having to spend a lot of time figuring it out.

If you're selling something, point out the main benefits for the audience, not just the features of the product or service. People want to know what's in it for them, and they don't want to slog through a lot of unnecessary details to get this information.

FRIENDLY ADVICE

Whether you're using text, images, or video, your message must be short and to the point. You have users' attention for just a few seconds, so make it count.

Standing Out from the Crowd

Facebook has millions of users, and millions of businesses are vying for their attention. That means you need to make yourself stand out from a lot of noise in order to get people to pay attention to your page.

When users do get to your page, you need to make sure that it stands out from other Facebook pages. Don't fall into the trap of making your page look like every other business. Spend some time and money creating a site that looks great, offers the fan a reason to return, and always contains engaging content and conversations.

In the following sections, we show you how to do this.

Getting the Creative Juices Flowing

In order for you to really set yourself apart on Facebook, you need to get creative and come up with some unique ideas. So it's time to start generating ideas for attention-grabbing campaigns.

If you ever get a creative block in coming up with ways to generate ideas, here are some tips:

- Unplug the computer
- Go for a walk
- Have a meeting outside
- Listen to music without words
- Doodle

Relying on computers stifles creativity. Often the best ideas come about when we put the electronic devices aside and just let the ideas flow.

Don't copy what everyone else is doing on Facebook. Worn-out ideas like giving away iPads get old really quickly and people just start to tune you out. Do things that others in your area of business haven't done before.

Thinking Strategically About Artwork

One of the biggest challenges with websites is that they are inherently driven by content, yet they need to be visually attractive, too.

Whether you're building out your Fan page or simply posting to your Wall, you should use pictures and images that resonate with your audience and drive them to take an action. That action may be to simply read your post or click on a link. The image serves primarily to get their attention.

FRIENDLY ADVICE

Make sure the artwork you use in your Facebook marketing campaigns is artwork that you own or is licensed for you to use.

You can purchase royalty-free artwork from any number of websites, including the following:

- iStockPhoto.com
- ShutterStock.com
- BigStockPhotos.com
- Corbis.com
- GettyImages.com

Having Crazy Fun

Social media and Facebook should be mostly about having fun. So when you're designing your Fan page, make sure you're working with fun, creative people who know how to make fans smile and laugh. If you're not having fun in your campaigns and conversations, you're not doing it right.

WATCH OUT

Too many people get into social media marketing and turn it into a new medium for technical support. While customer service is part of what you might provide, it shouldn't be the focus of your social media campaign.

Even seemingly "boring" businesses can have fun with their Facebook Fan page. For example, if you're a cardboard box manufacturer and you connect with users via Facebook, why not launch a contest for the most creative mascot for your company that's made exclusively out of boxes? Fans can submit photographs and videos of their mascot ideas. To get them thinking, you can post a few videos of your own:

- A kid dressed up in boxes as a robot

- Someone sliding down stairs in a box

- Neighborhood kids building box castles in their front yards

Are you feeling it? Do you see how fun this can be?

Launching Campaigns

When all of your artwork, media, and copy are in place, it's time to launch the campaign by using any of the tactics described earlier in this chapter.

Your next step is to set up an appropriate timeline and budget and track your campaigns.

Establishing a Timeline

Campaign timelines vary depending on your goals. The following table lists general time frames for various campaigns for maximum effectiveness.

Time Frames for Various Facebook Campaigns

Campaign	Time Frame
Contests	Two weeks
Facebook ads	Two to four weeks
Sponsored ads	One week or less
Wall posts and messages	Post every one to three days
Email marketing	One to two weeks

Sometimes situations arise that demand marketing campaigns be planned and launched in a short amount of time. When you're pressed for time, ads and Wall posts are the quickest ways to get your message out. But no matter how much pressure you're under to get your message out, always take the time to plan out your exact goals and use the most appropriate components for the campaign.

Setting a Budget

Your budget for your Facebook marketing campaigns depends on the size of your company, your goals, and how much money you have available. Some Facebook campaigns are free (aside for time and labor); others can add up quickly.

Here's a rundown of costs from least to most expensive:

- **Wall posts and messages:** No Facebook costs.

- **Email marketing:** No Facebook costs.

- **Facebook ads:** Fees range from inexpensive to very expensive depending on the keywords and demographics you choose. We have seen them range from 12¢ a click to over $3 a click on average.

- **Sponsored stories:** Sponsored stories cost slightly more than Facebook ads. We have seen them range from 50¢ a click to over $4 a click on average.

- **Unique page tabs:** Fees range from free to several thousand depending on the designers and the programmers you use.

Analyzing Your Campaign

After you've launched your campaign, take the time to analyze the data to see if it was effective.

Facebook Insights (see Figure 4.5) is a reporting tool that measures users' activity on your Fan page. It provides statistics on user demographics, Likes, and shares that occur on your Facebook page. (For details, see Chapter 16.)

WATCH OUT

Give yourself a good week or so when pulling statistics, and make sure you look at the dates carefully. Facebook introduces new features all the time, and Insights sometimes breaks down when it releases new updates. Check and analyze the data to make sure it makes sense.

In addition to Facebook Insights, you can use several tools to track the success of your Facebook campaigns. We recommend that you not only use Facebook Insights but also a website analytics package, like Google Analytics, and video stats, such as your YouTube Insights, as necessary.

Google Analytics is a free tool that allows you to track your website stats. This relates to Facebook in that you will be able to see how many visits come from your Facebook account. We describe how you set up this connection in Chapter 16.

If you're using videos on YouTube to integrate into your Facebook page, YouTube also has an Insights tool to give you metrics specific to the viewings of the videos.

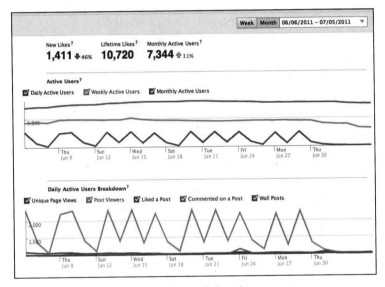

Figure 4.5: *Facebook Insights report.*

The Least You Need to Know

- If you're looking to get the most fans in the least amount of time, use Facebook ads.
- People want to know one thing in a Facebook marketing message: What's in it for me?
- If you're not having fun in your campaigns and conversations, you're not doing it right.
- Check and double-check your campaign before you launch it.
- Use Facebook Insights and other tracking tools to gauge the success of your campaigns.

The Voice of Your Business

In This Chapter

- Creating a Facebook persona
- Establishing your brand as an authority
- Aligning your team as one voice
- Developing content for Facebook
- Embodying your business voice in all of your marketing

The key to successfully marketing your business on Facebook is finding an authentic voice that connects with and engages your desired audience. This chapter walks you through some exercises to help you find and use your voice. Whether your business is small or large, we help you turn it into something fans will clamor to engage with.

Finding Your Voice

When people read your Facebook posts, they are not able to see your body language, which accounts for a large part of human communication. All they can go on are the words you use. Words can be tricky, and can have a variety of meanings depending on how they are used and by whom they are used.

Consider the comment, "I would like to get down."

By itself, this comment could mean many different things. It could mean a young child is standing on a ladder and wants to come down. It can mean a young woman wants to go out dancing with her friends. And it can mean an older man wants to lower his cholesterol.

The key here comes down to the person saying the words and in what tone. These physical attributes constitute the speaker's voice, and it's these attributes that you will visualize when you start communicating on Facebook.

Choosing a Celebrity Spokesperson

Think about a celebrity who represents the kind of energy and attitude that might translate well into a spokesperson for your business. Do you want your company to be as debonair as Sean Connery, as edgy and open as Betty White, or maybe as funny as Will Ferrell? Or perhaps you want to get a little nutty and go Charlie Sheen on your customers?

We're not talking about getting that exact celebrity to be your spokesperson—unless, of course, you can afford that in your budget. Instead, think about celebrities in terms of a *persona* that embodies your brand.

> **DEFINITION**
>
> A **persona** is a person's perceived personality.

We choose celebrities because they are so universally known, but you can certainly choose someone else whose persona you want to mimic.

Choosing a Role Model

For some companies, it makes more sense to mirror the voice of a role model from business, religion, or politics rather than a celebrity. Do you look to great leaders in your industry or others? What is it about them that you admire and want to replicate? Is it merely what they have been able to accomplish financially, or is it deeper? Do they have faith like no other and high integrity?

These same attributes apply as much to an individual as they do to a business on Facebook trying to find its voice. Many businesses can find their role model in successful executives of other companies. Consider business leaders like Jack Welch of GE, Michael Dell of Dell Computers, and Bill Gates of Microsoft. These leaders have a lot of admirable characteristics, and they are also celebrities of a sort.

Speaking Like an Authority

By this point, you should have a celebrity or leader in mind whose voice you want to imitate for your Facebook Fan page. Are you ready to start speaking like an authoritative celebrity? You're on your way to becoming a social media rock star.

Here are some tips to keep in mind:

- You are still your company, just presented with a unified voice.

- This voice shouldn't be totally new to your customers. It should represent the way that you do business.

- The most successful celebrities and role models have a lot of energy, which is part of what makes them so attractive to others. Find a way to generate the same level of energy.

FEEDBACK

An authority in business is rarely given that title. They generally just take it. It's kind of like power. Make yourself the authority of your niche. Use Facebook to do it.

So what does it mean to be an authority? It means all eyes and minds turn to you when you speak, post, and when others repost your information. Your word is law and people want to know all about anything you post.

Your Social Media Team as One Voice

After you've decided on a celebrity or role model whose voice you want to imitate, you need to get your entire team on board.

If some people on your team use the voice and others don't, the inconsistency weakens your brand. And a weak brand is one click away from invisible.

Modeling

To use a persona effectively on Facebook, you need to get into character. Think of yourself as an actor. Your goal is to live and breathe as the character you picked as the celebrity or role model.

What does the process entail? Watch a video or read a speech by the person you want to model. Pay attention to her every move. Notice what sets her apart and makes her special. Is it her body language? Her demeanor? Her tone?

For example, suppose you own a business where customers come to your house and you teach them how to cook, and you decide to embody the image of Julia Child. You likely value French cooking, are passionate about food, are approachable, and are genuinely funny. Translate these attributes into what you believe Julia Child would say about your business if she were managing your social media marketing.

Here are some posts you might use to promote your business when you adopt the voice of Julia Child.

- I've been rooting around in my icebox, and look what I found. Want to know? Come to my house. What fun we're going to have.

- It was a treat sharing my kitchen with my class last month. Come join me and we'll make the most delicious pig's and sheep's guts into delicacies.

- Do you tickle your lobsters like babies? *Bon appétit!*

- We're having a champagne and coffee party today in honor of the Queen of Sheba. Want to join us?

- *Bonjour!* Do you like French food? Tell me your favorite dish.

Acting Your Part

Getting into character before putting on a show is something that actors have been doing for years. We suggest you get into character before you write any content.

After you're in character, begin writing. We suggest devoting a few mornings to generating ideas and drafting the copy. People tend to be much fresher and creative in the morning than they are in the afternoon.

Take a cue from professional writers. Simply sit down in a comfortable place where you will not be disturbed, and write. Don't stop writing until your time is up. You might come up with a lot of information and ideas that you cannot and will not use, but you'll certainly end up with some content on which to build.

FEEDBACK

Put together a small manual and training program for your staff that clearly explains how to communicate the voice of social media. It will make the transition with newer employees easier for you in the future. In addition, keep track of all the messages, posts, and ads that you write for Facebook. These can serve as examples of your brand, which you can build on.

Moving from Voice to Content

Generating posts and replying back to fans in your celebrity or role model voice should be a fun task. Make sure to also use your persona as a directional tool to keep focused. Be strategic when creating content, using your voice as a tool but not going overboard with it.

Let's say you own a house painting company and decide that you want to use comedic actor Jack Black as your voice. Jack Black's personality can be described as nothing less than hilarious but full of heart. In order to start creating content, start with his personality as it talks about your business. A simple post might be, "What's black and white and red all over? If this describes your house, it's time for an upgrade."

Strategizing Your Posts

Your content shouldn't be what *you* think it should be. It should always be what your target market wants.

Too often, businesses treat Facebook like they treat their websites. The website approach is to tell people all about your business and why they should buy your products or services. On Facebook, it's okay to spend a little time doing this, but you should spend the majority of your time educating your fans with content that will benefit them.

If you own a landscape business, focus on offering tips on how to prepare the lawn for winter, how to get rid of grubs, and when to plant bulbs in your garden.

Dividing Your Content

Here's a guide for how you might want to divide your content:

- Educating (70%)
- Selling (15%)
- Fun (15%)

It's important to keep the selling and fun posts at just about equal amounts of content. This way your fans start to see the balance as equal and they always know that the bulk of what you offer is all about their needs, not yours.

Let's say you own a health food store and your target market is people interested in living a healthy, active lifestyle. Here is a sampling of posts that achieve a good balance of being informative/educational, more blatant sales calls, and just plain fun:

- Did you know that traditional methods of cooking vegetables causes them to lose up to 80 percent of their nutritional value?
- Healthy foods have a built-in reputation of being good for you but many have little or no taste. Spice is the answer.
- Cooking your food *al dente* retains the maximum number of nutrients and taste.
- The sweet potato makes a comeback as a popular food (and it's healthy, too!).
- Would you like to learn secrets for selecting, storing, and preparing healthy food?

The Art of Facebook Posting

Now that your voice is defined, and you've been introduced to a lot of Facebook posts, it's time to use that voice to turn up the heat in your Facebook posts to engage with your users.

Suppose that you're an online distributor of kitchen parts serving other businesses and you've chosen Will Ferrell as your celebrity voice. That means you need to get really punchy and funny while still getting a message across that will generate Likes and clicks to drive traffic to your Fan page.

Here are some ideas for using images and words:

Picture: An old oven next to a new-looking one.

Content: Both of these ovens are 3 years old. Want to know what the difference is? Go to PartsToYouFast.com.

Picture: A turtle with lettuce and tomato stuffed in the shell. Maybe a slice of cheese, too.

Content: In need of a new part for your broiler? Cheeseburgers cooking up too slow? Tommy the Turtle thinks so, too. Order from PartsToYouFast.com today.

Picture: An igniter for an oven.

Content: Time to rekindle that flame in your life? Learn about what prolongs igniters at the PartsToYouFast blog.

Picture: A piece of toast with clock parts on it.

Content: Need a part for your toaster oven and have no time to spare? Your order is always up at PartsToYouFast.com!

Picture: An oven that transforms into a robot with guns chasing people.

Content: Has your oven gone mad again? Don't worry. Call PartsToYouFast.com today and we'll get a replacement part out to you in no time.

Picture: An old advertisement for Spam.

Content: Have last-minute company coming for the weekend? Not sure what to cook? Keep cool—we have the answer.

Picture: A hamster clinging to a rope or a trapeze bar, looking down (scared).

Content: Tired of being put on hold when ordering replacement parts for your appliances? Order from PartsToYouFast.com and we won't leave you hanging.

Picture: A police vehicle with donuts for wheels.

Content: Today is June 3rd … National Donut Day. Go ahead. Take an extra coffee break and indulge.

Are you getting the hang of this yet?

Responding with a Smile

Being on the frontline of social media, you are the eyes, ears, and mouth of your business. One of the greatest skill sets you can develop is your customer service skill—giving your customers that little extra glimmer without seeming like a flirt.

I recently wanted to go to a local ice cream parlor and wasn't sure what they offered, so I looked up the business on Facebook and asked them what their specialty flavors were. Inadvertently, I mistyped my message to them and it came out: "What's your favorite flavor of ice?" Here is that encounter:

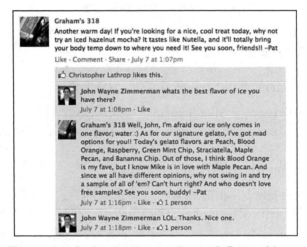

Figure 5.1: *Graham's 318 responding with flair and humor.*

They replied with a funny, punchy post (see Figure 5.1). It won me over and I went there for gelato.

Defining Your Business Brand

What defines your business brand today? You want to express your brand with positive words and messages, and by images and/or videos that convey the real nature of your purpose, value, and processes. While these are hard concepts to pin down, the first step in articulating your brand is to define the opposite attributes.

Here's an exercise to try right now. Take out a sheet of paper and write out adjectives that might hurt or damage your brand image. For example, here are some negative attributes you might want to avoid:

- Uncaring
- Apprehensive
- Uncertain
- Disconnected
- Reactive
- Rigid
- Complicated

Make sure that any messages you post on Facebook don't inadvertently convey these negative attributes. Doing so can seriously damage your brand.

Now write down adjectives that describe your business in a positive manner. Do these terms describe your business?

- Forward-thinking
- Expert
- Clear
- Value-driven

- Agile
- Concerned
- Together
- Confident
- Energetic
- Innovative

> **FRIENDLY ADVICE**
>
> Identifying and clearly communicating your brand to your staff is just as important as it is to the outside world. Your staff needs to have a firm grasp of your brand in order to generate marketing materials that fit with the image you want to instill in the minds of your customers.

The Least You Need to Know

- Choose a celebrity or role model personality to embody when writing content.
- Make sure all members of your social marketing team are trained in using the same, consistent voice. A hodge-podge of voices weakens your brand.
- Content should always be written based on the demands of the consumer, not necessarily what you think it should be.
- Your posts should contain about 15 percent humor and 15 percent selling. The rest should be valuable information for your target market.
- One of the greatest skill sets you can develop is your customer-service skills.

Your Business on Facebook

Big ideas are fine, but it's important to get your Facebook business page up, determine how to optimize the page, and tie down the basic details. This part has all you need to get up and running like the best of them, including how to set up your Facebook page, determining what kind of page to create, and establishing a strong presence from the start.

Creating Your Facebook Account

In This Chapter

- Getting on Facebook
- Setting up your shop
- Picking a good Profile picture
- Using storytelling to engage customers
- Building your Facebook brand

Before you can start marketing your business on Facebook, you need to set up your Facebook account and get your page up and running.

In this chapter, we step you through the process of setting up your Facebook presence. We then delve into the nitty-gritty of creating fruitful relationships and managing your Facebook image on a day-to-day basis.

It's Your Life on Facebook

Your Facebook page is like your virtual front office. You use it to accomplish the following tasks:

- Meet customers for the first time
- Manage customer compliments and complaints
- Create a positive public image
- Interact directly with the public

Notice what *isn't* on the list:

- Have company discussions
- Manage internal problems
- Handle major service issues

In other words, you shouldn't use Facebook to deal with the messy, complicated stuff related to the internal workings of your business. Instead, you want your customers to view your Facebook page as a map to find whatever it is they're looking for.

Are You on Facebook Yet?

Chances are you're one of the 800 million users already on Facebook. However, at this stage you may only have a personal account. Building a Facebook page for your business or brand is more complex than creating a personal Facebook page.

In fact, we recommend that you keep your personal and business Facebook pages separate. Your personal Facebook page should be where you post more intimate items, such as personal photos, political views, and religious beliefs. Your business page should focus on your products or services and offer information of value to users.

It may seem obvious that you should create a separate page for your business, but both John and Damon have seen plenty of examples where entrepreneurs tried to build their company presence on their personal pages.

For example, if you paint portraits in your spare time, your personal page is the perfect place to display your work and keep friends and family informed about your creative efforts. But if you start getting very popular, and you start selling enough paintings that you might be able to quit your day job and start painting full time, it's time to start thinking about creating a separate page for your work. Otherwise, before you know it hundreds of clients and fans of your work will friend you, and they will all have access to your personal information. If you create a separate business account for your portrait business, you can keep some separation between your personal life and your business life.

If you want to restrict someone's access to your personal page, you can limit the information shown to a particular person by putting him or her into a special category. For example, when you accept someone's friendship, you can create the Facebook category called "Business Associates" and prevent people in that category from seeing photos of your family or other personal information.

However, there are two reasons why you should still create a separate professional/ business page. First, if you truly want to connect with your customers, you want to give information, not censor information. Restrict access too much, and they'll be looking at virtually a blank page! Second, new friends can see what category they've been placed in. Some people may be offended that they are put in a category at all, especially if you're giving them limited information about you.

FRIENDLY ADVICE

Although you should feel free to link to your business page from your personal page, avoid linking from your business page to your personal page. You might lose potential customers because they don't like what they see on your personal page. For instance, a customer may decide not to purchase from you because of your political or religious beliefs. The higher your position in a company, the more you should consider keeping your personal Facebook page privacy settings high.

Setting Up Your Account

To set up your business page, open your web browser, go to www.facebook.com, and then click the **Create a Page** link (see Figure 6.1).

Sign Up

It's free and always will be.

First Name:

Last Name:

Your Email:

Re-enter Email:

New Password:

I am: Select Sex:

Birthday: Month: Day: Year:

Why do I need to provide my birthday?

Sign Up

Create a Page for a celebrity, band or business.

Figure 6.1: *The sign-up page on Facebook.*

Facebook prompts you to choose from among the following six categories (see Figure 6.2):

- **Local Business or Place:** Geared more toward small businesses and establishments.

- **Company, Organization, or Institution:** A great choice for corporations.

- **Brand or Product:** If your product or service is a bigger focus than the company itself, such as Coke's trademark soft drink or Harley-Davidson's iconic motorcycles.

- **Artist, Band or Public Figure:** The focus here is on a person or group of people.

- **Entertainment:** Public venues such as movie theaters or dance clubs usually grab this type of page.

- **Cause or Community:** Focused on nonprofit, fundraising, or awareness items.

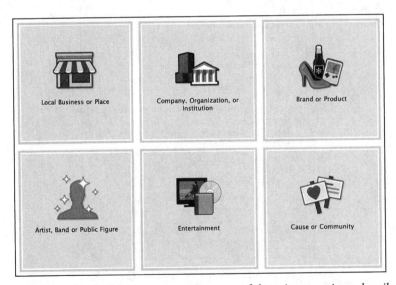

Figure 6.2: *Facebook prompts you to choose one of these six categories to describe your business.*

Choose the category that best describes your business. Facebook asks you for a specific set of information based on your choice. For instance, if you select **Local Business or Place**, Facebook prompts you to indicate the type of business or place, its name, and its contact information.

Facebook then asks you for your email address and whether or not you currently have a Facebook account. If you don't have an account, you can create one at this time.

Next, we look at the details you want to fill out before your Facebook business page goes live.

Creating a Facebook Brand

Here are things to consider as you look at the big-picture marketing plan.

Storytelling

If your company or brand were a living, breathing thing—which we think it virtually is!—then your Facebook page is the day-to-day or week-to-week chronicle of its life. Your customers, fans, and followers are interested enough in it to give your business some of their precious attention. They want to hear the story of your business.

When we talk about storytelling, we don't mean John Grisham novels. We mean showing your customers what your business is really about.

One excellent example of this is Southwest Airlines. The popular airline not only uses its Facebook page to promote its latest fares, but it also gives readers an inside peek into their business. For instance, to celebrate its fortieth anniversary in June 2011, Southwest posted classic videos and fun facts about the company on its Facebook page.

Good storytelling rewards current customers for their loyalty and brings on board new customers who are interested in hearing more from you.

Your Profile Picture

It may seem like a minor detail, but your Profile picture is a crucial element of your Facebook page. When you do a search on Facebook for, say, "cookies," all the businesses are listed with minimum info—and a big picture. For many customers, the picture is their first impression—and everyone knows how important first impressions are!

When deciding on a Profile picture, keep these guidelines in mind:

- **Make sure it's in line with your company's philosophy and goals.** A picture of the family that owns the business may be appropriate for, say, a law firm, but it would make little sense for a motorcycle company or a large corporation.

- **Keep it simple.** It should look good both in mobile phones and home computers.

- **Use a consistent image.** If you have a well-established logo, use it unless cycling different pictures is a part of your marketing plan.

> **FRIENDLY ADVICE**
>
> Keep your Profile picture consistent across all your social media marketing campaigns. When creating your Facebook pic, think about how it will look on Twitter, LinkedIn, and other sites as well as on your official website.

- **Hire a professional photographer or artist.** It's worth it to spend a couple hundred or even a couple thousand dollars for a high-quality image that represents your business.

Other Details

Facebook asks you to fill in the following details as you set up your account: To fill or edit this information, click **Edit Page** in the right column (see Figure 6.3).

- **Your Settings:** How you'd like to post news on your Facebook Wall and how you'd like to be contacted by Facebook regarding your account (see Figure 6.4).

- **Manage Permissions:** How much freedom visitors will have to post on your company's Facebook Wall.

- **Basic Information:** The bio, contact info, and other details about your company.

- **Profile Picture:** The option to upload a picture representing your business.

- **Featured:** The option to highlight a particular news item or graphic on the page.

- **Resources:** Links to helpful Facebook tips and tricks.

- **Manage Admins:** Decide who will have the power to edit the Facebook page.

- **Apps:** The list of applications connected to your business page. By default, it includes photos, links, events, notes, and video.

- **Mobile:** Information on Facebook Mobile.

- **Insights:** Statistics on your visitors, page views, and other data.

- **Help:** Assistance with technical errors.

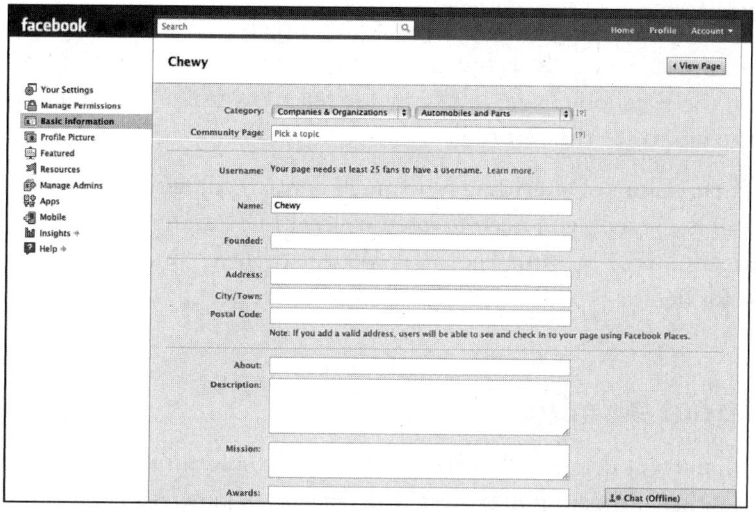

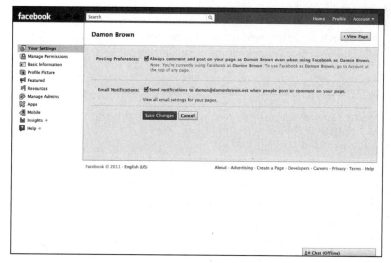

Figure 6.3: *Filling out info on the company page.*

Figure 6.4: *In Your Settings, you can determine your posting preferences and how Facebook notifies you.*

Don't worry: you don't have to enter everything right now and, based on customer feedback, you'll be tweaking things anyway. Aside from the Profile picture, however, you definitely need to knock out the following key details:

- **Contact info:** We know, you already entered your location when you created your account, but you can get even more detailed here. For instance, if you have a mobile business, you may want to include your cell phone number along with the office number.

- **Bio:** Keep your company or brand bio precise, focused, and short. Try to limit it to 30 words so the entire description fits under your Profile picture on the Facebook page; if it's any longer, most users won't bother to click on the bio to see the rest of it.

- **Permissions:** Determine how much control you want to give your visitors and how much you need to keep yourself. For example, do you want to let visitors write on your Facebook Wall without your signing off? (See Chapter 8 for details.)

A Word About Admins

The last important detail is choosing your *admin*, or administrator, for the account. This person has ultimate power over your Facebook page. You can choose more than one person to serve as the admin.

DEFINITION

An **admin** is the person who has control over the Facebook page. He or she can add, delete, or modify any information on the page.

Your admin will be able to take the following actions:

- Add or remove members or other admins from the page

- Delete content from the Wall

- Modify the official business information

- Change the pictures and other details

WATCH OUT

Having multiple admins for your business page is a double-edged sword. On one hand, it's nice to have two or three people be able to modify the page as opposed to having one person with all the power. On the other hand, if the multiple admins disagree on an action, having all of them "in charge" could lead to some serious drama. Choose wisely.

Managing a Facebook page can be a time-consuming process, so it is understandable that you may not want or be able to be admin. If you do have someone fill the role of admin, though, choose someone whom you trust.

Getting Personal in Business

Traditional marketing is like a one-way conversation: no matter how strong your message, you're always the one doing all the talking. Facebook, like other social media, is different. Marketing on Facebook is more like a mutual, intimate conversation with potential customers, current customers, and even former customers.

Just like in any other social situation, you need to know who to talk to, what to say, and what not to say. Understanding your relationship with your customers pays serious dividends.

Who to Talk to

Facebook offers a rare opportunity to interact with the following audiences:

- Current customers
- Potential customers
- Former customers
- Your competition's customers

FRIENDLY ADVICE

You can't be everything to everyone, so prioritize which group is your main audience. Focus on your main audience while keeping the other audiences in mind.

You can reach a whole cadre of Facebook users who aren't your customers but who might still be valuable to your business. These audiences include the following:

- Media

- Competitive businesses

- Complementary businesses

What to Say

Customers expect any business with a social media page to interact with them. In fact, a big reason why people love social media is because they feel a closer connection to their favorite celebrities, brands, and companies. You are expected to interact.

You should tailor what you say, and how often you say it, to the relationship you'd like to have with your consumer. For instance, the high-end couture house Prada would never post a daily Facebook message announcing that it's slashing prices on its pricey clothes and accessories. That's because it wants customers to view its products as luxury items—not things you just grab en masse, like toilet paper, when they happen to be on sale. Instead, Prada's best plan of attack would be occasional, perfectly phrased messages about, say, socialite Paris Hilton carrying its purse or the latest line shown at New York Fashion Week.

When you think about your message, consider the following issues:

- What your audience needs to hear

- What you need your audience to know

- How often they need to hear your message

- Which type of messaging—text, video, or web links—your audience is most responsive to

For example, if you run a local bank and are launching a new type of savings account, you need to tell your audience that the new product is available and point out the advantages of using the new product. If you're only offering the account for a limited time, you should be more aggressive about how many messages you send. And, being thoughtful about the content, you could include video with a customer showing how to sign up for the service or live web links that allow customers to sign up online immediately.

What Not to Say

You should avoid certain discussions on Facebook and have a plan to neutralize them if they do occur. The rub is that Facebook is a public forum: anything that anyone says on your Facebook page will be seen by all of your Facebook fans. You should always think carefully about what conversations you initiate and how you respond to particular situations.

Here are some topics to avoid—or if they can't be avoided, at least squashed—on your Facebook page:

- Racist, sexist, or other judgmental remarks

- Shouting matches between or with visitors

- Negative comments/discussions about competing products or services

You obviously want to avoid offending people with judgmental remarks, but the last two points are a little more complicated. Let's break them down a bit.

You're virtually guaranteed to have a few shouting matches between visitors on your Facebook page. And the more passionate your customers are about your product or service, the more likely they'll be to disagree with someone else—and vocalize that disagreement on your site.

When you see an argument beginning to build, try to determine if the flare-up will burn itself out. If the conversation only has a few passionate responses, or if nobody has responded to the conversation for a day or two, it's probably going to fade away on its own. Generally, the faster the responses come in, the more likely the conversation will flare up and get out of hand.

If the argument doesn't appear to be waning on its own, you absolutely have to intervene. Try humor ("Boy, you guys are really passionate about our ice cream!"), mediating ("It sounds like you agree to disagree, but both of you are right because …"), or even mock fame ("Here's to the two most loyal Damon's Ice Cream customers, Jack and Paul."). You'll make mistakes, but the biggest mistake you can make is letting two (or more) people hijack your brand's Facebook page.

In early 2011, Arizona State Representative Gabrielle Giffords was shot along with 19 others at a public speaking engagement. She survived, but the assassination attempt had some blowback on former Alaska Governor Sarah Palin. Prior to and during the shooting, Palin had a Facebook page with a U.S. map and gun sights on all the Democratic representatives' districts—including Giffords'.

Using the gun sights wasn't Palin's biggest mistake, though. By the end of the day of the shooting, Palin's team had removed all traces of the map from all her social media, including Facebook. At the same time, Palin was saying that the map was pure symbolism. Unfortunately, nothing can truly be erased from social media: the press discovered the deletions, they recovered the images, and they came at Palin even more aggressively for attempting to cover it up.

The lesson is to be gentle with that Delete button! Removing offending or embarrassing posts can have a bigger fallout than the posts themselves. You're better off addressing the material openly rather than covering it up.

You also need to be careful when users discuss competing products or services. Badmouthing other businesses is obviously a risky marketing strategy, but there are two nuances to consider.

First, don't be the one to initiate the badmouthing. For instance, a customer may say "Your ice cream is the best—way better than John's nasty cones!" It's easy to fall into this trap because it's a putdown (of a competitor) wrapped in a complement (of your brand). Respond carefully, saying something like "We're sure John works hard, too, and we're really happy you love our cones!"

Second, the same competitor you put down on your Facebook page might end up being a collaborator later. Facebook gives you the opportunity to destroy potential relationships as much as it gives you the chance to create them.

The Least You Need to Know

- As you set up your page, think about your audience, what they want to hear, and what you need to convey.
- Keep your Profile picture clean, simple, and professional-looking. It should be simple and easy to see in both small and large formats. You should strongly consider hiring a professional to create it for you.

- Be sure to include a brief bio and detailed contact info for your business.
- Snuff out inappropriate conversations before they get out of hand.
- Don't condone badmouthing of competitors on your Facebook page.

Facebook Fan Pages

In This Chapter

- Creating a Fan page
- Getting to know the Like button
- Distinguishing between Fan pages and other Facebook pages
- Visiting great Fan pages

Setting up a generic business page is one thing, but Facebook really lets you create a unique experience for your customers. We chat about great examples from big business and even small, local establishments later in the chapter.

For now, the first big step is deciding what kind of business page to create. A great option is a Fan page.

In this chapter, we fill you in on why you'd want a Fan page, show you how to create one, and give you tips for keeping it fresh and exciting.

Build It and They Will Come?

As the name suggests, Fan pages were originally made for celebrities like teen heart-throb Justin Bieber. But then a few savvy businesses started adopting Fan pages for their own brands, and since then they've evolved into a powerful marketing tool. Whether used for celebrities like Justin Bieber or as marketing tools for businesses, Facebook calls all of them Fan pages.

A Fan page connects you with your customers, but those connect with you not by friending you (as with regular Facebook pages), but by Liking you. When you create a Fan page and place the Like button on the internet, any Facebook user can instantly say she is interested in your brand by clicking **Like**. A Like is the Facebook equivalent of signing up for a mailing list: once someone Likes you, he or she receives a notice every time you update your Fan page with new content.

WATCH OUT

People can "Unlike" your business just as quickly as they can Like it—it's just a matter of them clicking a button. A bad interaction with your company, shoddy products, or other negative experiences can cause a customer to Unlike you in a heartbeat. Keep your customer in mind or your Likes can drop sharply!

The following sections walk you through the process of setting up a Fan page. It may not end up being your cup of tea compared to the more organized Group page (see Chapter 8), but feel free to give it a shot—you can always delete it before it goes live.

Setting Up Your Fan Page

If you've already set up your business page (see Chapter 6), then you already have a Fan page—remember that Facebook doesn't distinguish between whether the Fan page is for a pop star or a corporation. Head to www.facebook.com and click **Create a page**:

1. Open your web browser

2. Go to www.facebook.com

3. Click **Create a page**

Be sure you are looking at the Facebook front page, not your Facebook page. If you are just seeing your information, you are logged in to Facebook. Log out and you'll see the actual Facebook front page.

You will see six different categories:

- Local Business or Place

- Company, Organization, or Institution

- Brand or Product

- Artist, Band or Public Figure

- Entertainment

- Cause or Community

These are all Fan pages! Users can Like every one of these types of pages. And they have the added bonus of being the easiest kind of business pages to get started.

Choosing a Name

When choosing a title for your Fan page, be as clear as possible, for a number of reasons:

- **Your Fan page name appears on your Like button, and Like buttons can float anywhere on the internet:** For instance, a loyal customer may put your Facebook Like button on his website. The twist is that the Like button will only list a couple words from your Fan page name. If the name of your business is Manny Snuffalupogas Jr.'s Pizzeria, you probably want to call your page Manny Jr.'s Pizza or another abbreviated title.

FRIENDLY ADVICE

Chances are you've seen Facebook's Like thumbs up symbol on an online restaurant menu, a musician's music page, a museum website, or any other stand-alone site—anywhere but Facebook itself. You're going to want to put the Like icon on all of your multimedia correspondence online. More importantly, you want others to have an easy time putting a Like button for your service on their page. Make the name clear and concise so it can stand alone, no matter where it's located.

- **Good terms maximize searchability:** Google, Yahoo!, and other internet search engines look for simple, clear terms. The clearer the term, the more likely it will recommend a website to a user. "San Francisco auto repair" will be recommended sooner than "SF auto" or "Bay cars," since the latter terms don't include enough context.

- **Simpler names are easier to remember:** The Fan page for Coca-Cola is simply called "Coca-Cola," not "Coca-Cola Awesome Facebook Page!" or "The Best Soda In The World."

WATCH OUT

You can't go back and rename your Fan page at a later time, so choose your name wisely and be sure to double-check the spelling and punctuation before clicking **Accept**.

Creating Custom Tabs

Custom Facebook tabs are additional page tabs that you can add to your Facebook Fan page. The links to these pages appear on the left side of the page under your Profile picture or logo.

You might want to create these for any of the following reasons:

- To add an area for more content and promotion

- To add a page where you can collect information from your fans, such as their contact information

- To conduct contests

- To enliven your Fan page to be much more than a Wall

You have many options for creating custom Fan page tabs. Here we show you how to use a free application, Static HTML: iframe tabs, for creating custom tabs.

Here's what you do:

1. Search for "Static HTML: iframe tabs" in the Facebook Search field.

2. Find the app, and select it. (To make sure you select the one we are referencing, as of October 2011, this app has over 60,694,000 monthly active users and that is noted on the app page. If you reach a page that has fewer users, it's not the app we're talking about.)

3. Click **Go to App** at the top of the page (see Figure 7.1).

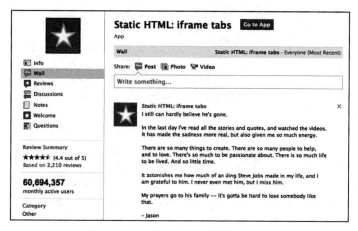

Figure 7.1: *The Static HTML page.*

4. Select the page you want to install this app on. Use the drop-down menu and find your page, then click the **Add Static HTML: iframe tabs** link (see Figure 7.2).

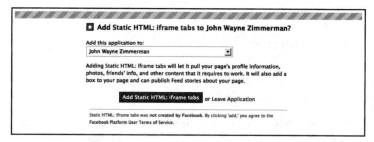

Figure 7.2: *Adding the Static HTML app to Facebook.*

5. Your Fan page displays. From here, click the **Edit Page** link.

6. Click the **Apps** link. This shows you all the apps you have installed on your page (see Figure 7.3). Find and click the **Static HTML: iframe tabs**.

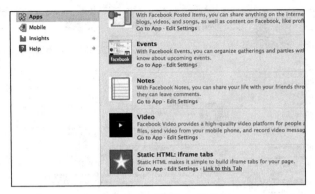

Figure 7.3: *The list of apps, with Static HTML now at the bottom.*

7. This app has three links that allow you to create more custom tabs, remove the custom tab from your page, and show you the direct link to the tab:

Use **Go to App** to go back to the main app page and install another tab. Typically, the first tab you want to create is a Welcome custom tab (see Figure 7.4), but you may want to come back to this link later and create a tab for products, a tab for customer support, or anything else that you want to showcase on your Facebook page.

Use **Edit Settings** to add or remove the tab from the left menu on your page, or to name the tab. Click on the link, and select the Add/Remove links as necessary. To change the title of your tab, just type in the name you want to display in the left menu in the text box.

Use **Link to this Tab** to show the permanent link to your tab. You can copy and paste the link that is displayed, which you can place in emails, on your website, or in Wall posts.

Figure 7.4: *Click on the Welcome link for Static HTML.*

8. Click **View Page**. The new tab displays in the left menu. Click the tab.

9. A screen displays with two comment boxes (see Figure 7.5). In the first box, you enter content using HTML, CSS, JavaScript, or any other content you can use on a regular webpage. Fans and nonfans can see the content in the top box. Any content that you add to the bottom box can be viewed by fans only. You can choose to leave the box blank. If you use the bottom box, after users click **Like**, the screen changes to the content in the bottom box.

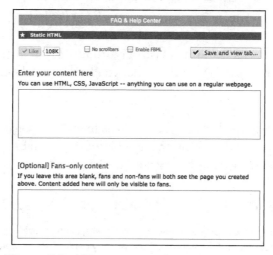

Figure 7.5: *Adding content to your new Fan page tab.*

10. When you are finished pasting your content into either or both comment boxes, click the **No scrollbars** checkbox at the top of this page. Leave the Enable FBML box unchecked. (FBML is Facebook markup language that is being phased out of Facebook.)

11. Click **Save and view tab** (see Figure 7.6).

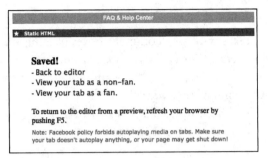

Figure 7.6: *Saving your content on Facebook.*

12. The Saved! window displays (see Figure 7.6). From here, you can go back to edit your new page(s), or view what you have created either as a fan or as a nonfan.

You now have a custom tab. Feel free to add as many additional tabs as you like. However, we recommend limiting the number of custom tabs to five so you don't overwhelm fans with your marketing messages.

WATCH OUT

Don't automatically play any media on your tabs, such as a video. Facebook has a rule against this, and if you break the rule, they could close your account.

Creating Wild Fans

Here's a secret: people actually want to Like your business. At the end of the day, consumers want reliable producers, consistent brands, and great service. When they find it, they support it.

We assume you're doing the very best you can with your business, so that part is covered. Now you just need to get your business in front of the right people's faces. Your Facebook Fan page is the bridge between you and your next customer.

WIIFM

When it comes to customers, "What's In It For Me?", or *WIIFM*, is the main thing they care about. The more quickly you can make clear to them the advantages of working with your business, the faster they will listen—and maybe even purchase your product or service.

> **DEFINITION**
>
> **WIIFM,** short for "What's In It For Me?", means that people are more likely to do something for you if it clearly will be beneficial to them.

In traditional sales, WIIFM usually involves convincing someone that buying your service will be in their best interest. In social media marketing—and Facebook marketing in particular—the conversation doesn't end when customers drive the proverbial car off the lot.

With a Facebook Fan page, the conversation with the consumer continues after the initial sale, as he or she is able to communicate with you about problems with the product, questions about the service, or even references for other potential customers. All the while, WIIFM will have to be paramount in your mind. Here are some tips:

- Don't just tell customers to "Like our page!" Instead, give them an incentive to Like the page, such as exclusive sales, discounts, or other valuable information.

- Keep content on your Fan page fresh so customers will have incentive to visit regularly and also share your news on their own Facebook page.

- Include all your relevant content information on the Fan page, from customer help lines to all your locations, so customers begin viewing your page as a resource.

Broadcast vs. Interaction

Facebook marketing turns a one-directional campaign into a two-way conversation. However, it's up to you how much you'd like your business to interact with customers. We call it a case of broadcast versus interaction. Here are some examples:

Broadcast	Interaction
Telling followers you're having a sale	Asking followers what they'd like to see on sale and responding accordingly
Posting a customer hotline	Addressing customer concerns directly through the Facebook page
Telling customers about changes	Showing customers why changes in policy, procedure, or practice are taking place and including them in the conversation
Showing the latest advertisement exclusively on the Facebook page	Asking visitors to vote for their favorite ad

Interaction gives users an incentive to come back. The downside is that it requires a much bigger time commitment than broadcasting.

WATCH OUT

It's better to be low-key and consistent than to be overambitious and unstable. If some weeks you post a lot of content to your page and then let weeks go by without posting anything, customers may view your business as flaky and unreliable. And be sure to ration your resources to allow for a consistent marketing campaign. In other words, don't plan a spectacular, interactive December, and have absolutely no resources left to follow up your interactivity in January.

Think about your long-term financial, time, and manpower resources before you push for more interaction on your Fan page.

Domino's Pizza is one of our favorite cases of broadcast versus interaction. The successful food chain had its 50th anniversary in 2010—and had some of the worst customer feedback compared to its competitors. For CEO Patrick Doyle, the breaking point was receiving a photo from a customer of a delivered pizza: The Domino's Pizza driver was so sloppy and the toppings were so loose, the pizza toppings smashed up against the top of the box. The carelessness was starting to affect Domino's Pizza's sales, too.

The CEO had had enough. In 2010, he started the "We Suck!" campaign, where customers were encouraged to post pictures of Domino's Pizza's screw-ups. Wrong toppings, burnt pizzas—anything that the company messed up. He said that his company had to do better, and the only way that was going to happen would be if everyone was held accountable. It was, of course, part of a multi-million-dollar ad campaign, but customers seemed to appreciate the honesty, too: Domino's Pizza sales went up 16 percent, a serious number for a worldwide corporation.

Beyond the honesty, though, Domino's Pizza pushed its customers to participate in the revitalization of its brand. By using Facebook and other social media, the company made an impact not by broadcasting, but by interacting.

Checking Out Some of the Best Fan Pages

As you can imagine, Facebook has millions of Fan pages. Most of them are not exemplary. However, some of them have a great mix of interaction and broadcasting, and personality and service.

The following sections show you a few Fan pages worth Liking on Facebook.

Big Brands

When it comes to Facebook marketing, don't envy the biggest brands. The bar is much higher for Burger King or Citibank to create a cool, interactive experience than it is for your local burger joint or small-town bank. And if these big-brand companies screw up on the social media front, their failures get a lot of attention from the media, competitors, and, most importantly, potential and current customers.

There are several reasons why it can be more difficult for big brands to make their mark on Facebook:

- They often have multi-million-dollar budgets, so the pressure to create something spectacular is higher.

- They are less likely to do something interesting or daring because of financial risk, corporate conservatism, or other issues.

- If they screw up on the social media front, their failures are noticed more by media, competitors, and potential and current customers.

The soda company Coca-Cola represents itself very well on Facebook at www. facebook.com/cocacola. However, the company presents some real challenges for harnessing Facebook's social networking powers. For one thing, there's the product problem: no one is going to order a bottle of Coke online, so the company's Facebook strategy can't be to just slap a "Buy Now" button on its page and call it a day. And Coke is almost too well known of a brand for anyone to bother to Like its Coca-Cola Fan page. The average person knows what Coke's famous recipe tastes like, most Americans grew up watching Coke commercials, and the logo is as familiar as Mickey Mouse's ears and McDonald's golden arches.

The company made the following good social-marketing decisions when they created their Facebook page:

- They focus on the brand, not the drink.

- They showcase fan-created media, honoring their customers and tapping into original, homemade content.

- They provide links to Twitter, YouTube, and the photo service Flickr. Potential customers can use whatever social media service they feel most comfortable with.

FEEDBACK

In August 2008, the web company Dusty and Michael noticed that Coca-Cola didn't have a Facebook presence. The two guys from Los Angeles decided to create a Facebook Fan page for their favorite soda.

Coca-Cola noticed, liked what it saw, and asked the guys if they would mind turning the page into the official Coca-Cola Fan page. Now working for Coke, Dusty and Michael's original page is the foundation of what is online today. The duo regularly posts updates and has had an ongoing viral video series showcasing their adventures on the road with Coke.

The page is less about pushing soda and more about creating a community of people who happen to really like drinking Coke. The soft drink conglomerate ends up coming off hipper than most companies a fraction of its size.

Medium-Sized Brands

Medium-sized businesses may have the toughest time making an impression. Here are some reasons why:

- They lack the resources of a big brand.

- They have less brand recognition compared to bigger brands, which means they may have to work harder to get a Facebook Like than other companies.

- They don't have the notoriety or newness of a scrappy startup.

- They may be stuck in transition between being a small company and a large brand, giving it the strength of neither and the weaknesses of both.

The stationary manufacturer Livescribe, a mid-size company, has a particularly compelling Fan page (see Figure 7.7). Livescribe sells pens that enable you to record your conversation while simultaneously writing down notes.

Figure 7.7: *The Livescribe Fan page.*

The smartly designed Livescribe Fan page provides visitors with plenty of information about the company and its products. Along the left side of the page are direct links for accessing the company's newest information, connecting via other platforms like Twitter, and—of course—buying the pen and its accessories.

The main area features videos that show the pen in action—a crucial step for an unusual product like Livescribe. In that sense, both Livescribe and the big brand Coca-Cola have the same issue: How do you show someone something that you have to experience? You can't try a Livescribe pen online, just like you can't taste a Coke through Facebook. Multimedia, like videos in the case of Livescribe, can truly save the day. Imagine how difficult describing a product like Livescribe would be without internet platforms like Facebook!

Fans can also engage in community discussions and are encouraged to share content and details that facilitate bonding between users. The more Livescribe users feel like a community, the more likely they will come back to the page to socialize, not to mention buy more products.

Small Businesses

Believe it or not, small businesses harness Facebook for the biggest advantages.

- Because of their size, they're more likely to value each and every customer, and that level of engagement means more loyal visitors—which translates into more Likes.

- They are also unlikely to fall under as much scrutiny as larger companies, so they have more room to experiment and find the right social media rhythm.

- They often are more determined to push the boundaries of what's possible simply because, unlike larger companies, no one is telling them "No, we can't do that" or "No, because we've never done that before."

- With the low barrier to entry, Facebook evens the playing field between small companies and their larger counterparts.

The San Francisco–based ice cream shop Bi-Rite Creamery has a Facebook page worth visiting (see Figure 7.8). At first glance, it looks almost exactly like a standard Facebook personal page. Except for its prominent logo, it doesn't feature any original graphics or heavy visuals.

Take a good look, though. Notice the spread of pictures across the top. From the visuals, all the pictures are of the tasty ice cream and regular-looking folks enjoying it. The simple layout and warm pics contribute to the local, small-business feel.

Also, note the conversation taking place with the Bi-Rite Creamery audience. On Father's Day week, Bi-Rite asks, "What's the best gift you've ever given your dad? (edible or not!)" Fans responded with funny, interesting answers. Bi-Rite Creamery's Fan page is engaging because of its simplicity and seemingly open line to the owners.

Figure 7.8: *The Bi-Rite Creamery Facebook Fan page.*
(Courtesy of Bi-Rite Creamery)

What All Successful Brands Have in Common

Coca-Cola, Livescribe, and Bi-Rite Creamery show how big, medium, and small companies can take advantage of Facebook. However, as you may notice, all three of the companies follow certain common strategies:

- They interact rather than broadcast.
- Their pages reflect their customers' values and interests.
- They focus on the brand, not the product.
- They create a community—a reason for the visitor to come back—and assume that the sales will naturally come later.
- They are selling products that can't even be tried online, such as ice cream, digital pens, and soft drinks.

The strengths and challenges of a small, medium, or large business using Facebook are unique, but the basic rules apply to virtually any company. There's no excuse for you not to take advantage of Facebook's Fan pages.

The Least You Need to Know

- Facebook Fan pages were originally made for celebrities, but now businesses make the most use of Fan pages.
- When someone Likes your Fan page, he or she gets a notice every time you update it.
- WIIFM, or "What's In It For Me?", is a marketing approach in which you make sure your potential customers know there is a benefit involved for individuals who become your customers.
- Small businesses have advantages over big ones when it comes to using Facebook as a marketing tool.

Facebook Group Pages

In This Chapter

- Creating a Group page
- Choosing between Fan and Group pages
- Determining who gets into your group
- Moderating group discussion
- Controlling the flow of information

If Fan pages (see Chapter 7) are the come-one, come-all gathering spots, then Group pages are the exclusive, velvet-rope clubs. The biggest benefit of a Group page is that you can tailor each visitor's experience more than you can with a Fan page. The biggest challenge is successfully using that control to benefit both your customer and your brand.

In this chapter, we talk about starting a group, determining its parameters, and curating the experience once you get it up and running. With this knowledge under your belt, you'll be able to determine what kind of Facebook page—Fan page or Group page—is best for your business.

When Fan Pages Don't Cut It

Remember how people get onto your Fan page? They simply click a **Like** icon and, voilà, they're suddenly on your virtual mailing list.

Unfortunately, Fan pages don't offer much insight into who these people are or whether or not they like your product—they could have hit your **Like** link by mistake or because a friend did! Fan pages are definitely the way to go if you're interested purely in numbers, but sometimes you want to create a community with a little more finesse. This is when a *Group page* comes in handy.

Joining a Facebook Group isn't as simple as clicking a Like button. It can be as sophisticated as getting an invite to a private club or as simple as meeting certain group qualifications. And the group organizer has the right to refuse people membership or even kick people out of the club.

On a Group page, the admin—more than likely you—determines the group's dynamics. Facebook lets users create the following three types of Facebook Groups:

- Hidden
- Closed
- Open

Your visitor's experience changes dramatically depending on the type of group. The following sections describe each type of group in detail.

Hidden Groups

When a group is hidden, it doesn't appear on any search list. You actually need to know about it and directly type in the group name in order to find it.

On Facebook, go to the search bar at the top of the screen and begin typing in a word like, say, "McD." Facebook autofills the search box and suggests several, if not dozens of, pages you may be looking for (in this example, the majority of suggestions would be McDonald's pages; see Figure 8.1). A search like this is an easy way to find a group of your interest.

Figure 8.1: *Facebook autofills your search bar.*

FRIENDLY ADVICE

Hidden groups tend to have fewer members compared to a Fan page or even an invite-only group. However, the low number of members means that the people who are in it feel special. The more special they feel, the more likely they'll be to express their loyalty to your brand—monetarily or otherwise.

A hidden group can give the air of exclusivity and mystery, two feelings that could work well with the right brand. For example, a hip college radio station may have a significant following in the real world, but only the coolest kids know about the Facebook group hiding in plain sight. You can imagine that the conversations, camaraderie, and even competition among members would be higher on such a page than it would be on a Fan page.

Closed Groups

You don't need to hide your group to keep it exclusive. Instead, you can make the group invite-only by choosing the Closed privacy setting. The name of a closed group shows up when you perform a search for it, but only members are able to see the contents.

You can manage closed groups in two ways: you can give clearance on every new member, or you can empower members themselves to bring in new people. Both approaches have their pros and cons.

> **FEEDBACK**
>
> You can change the type of group at any time—from closed to open, for example. However, we caution against making too many changes after your Group page is up and running because you always want to present a consistent identity of your business.

If you retain the power over giving clearance on every member, you can handpick who you'd like to be in the club. Unfortunately, handpicking takes a lot of time and effort. If your page takes off the way you're hoping it does, you would have to dedicate serious resources to deciding on new members, an amount of work that could get even more concerning as the group gets more popular and more people ask to join.

Letting members vouch for new members builds up trust in the community and takes the pressure off of you to manage initial membership. The challenge is that, by giving up some power, the members may end up co-signing people who are toxic to your group. In other words, you have to monitor new members anyway.

Open Groups

The simplest approach is to make your group open to the public. Sounds just like a Fan page, right? They're very similar.

A key difference between the open-by-default Fan page and the open Group page is that the Group page enables you to contact all members directly and simultaneously. We get into group communications later in the chapter.

Setting Up Your Group

To set up a group, log in to your Facebook account. In the left column is a list of any groups you belong to. At the end of the list, click the **Create Group** link.

In the Create Group window that displays (see Figure 8.2), type the name of your group in the Group Name field. Be certain that the name you pick is the name you really want, because you can't change the name. We recommend that you give your group a unique title so it doesn't get lost in the mix. For instance, if you want to create a group about pumpkin farms, don't just call it "pumpkin farms." Use your name as a branding tool. You could call it, "John's Largest List of Pumpkin Farms on the Planet."

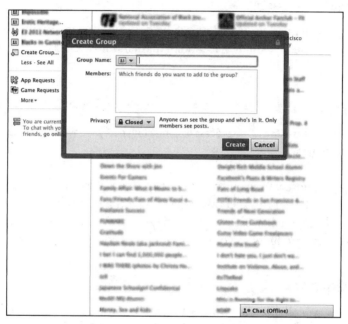

Figure 8.2: *The Create Group window prompts you to enter a group name and choose members.*

In the Members field, choose which Facebook friends, if any, you'd like to invite. Finally, in the Privacy drop-down menu, select whether you want the group to be hidden, closed, or open. You can edit other details after you launch your page, but this is enough to get the group started.

Build Them Bigger and Faster

Groups give you the ability to create a tight community faster than Fan pages. Group pages also make it much easier to communicate with members.

United Messaging

One of the biggest advantages groups have over Fan pages is that you can contact the whole group quickly. With Like-driven Fan pages, your latest page updates are thrown in with the rest of a fan's News Feed. If the fan happens to miss your notice, she doesn't get the message.

However, groups let you do *united messaging* directly into the mailboxes of everyone in the group. You send a single Facebook email and it reaches every member of the group.

> **DEFINITION**
>
> **United messaging** is the process of contacting everyone within a group with a single email.

For instance, suppose you want to tell your group about a new line of products you're launching this Fall. Go to Facebook Email, type the group name, and create your message. You have quick access to everyone in your group! You can even attach pictures of your new products to your messages or send along information sheets.

Group Documents

One great way to collaborate within a Facebook Group is by creating a group document. Why make an item available within the group? It's an excellent way to collaborate on a specific document. Here's how you do it:

1. Go to your group page.

2. Click **Create a Doc** on the right column.

3. Type in the document title and body.

4. Click Create Doc in the upper-right corner (see Figure 8.3).

Facebook makes the document available for the group to read and edit.

Figure 8.3: *Creating a group document.*

Facebook Doc has several features similar to a basic word processing program such as Microsoft Word. Starting from the left, the icons are as follows:

- Bold

- Italic

- Numbered list

- Bulleted list

- Add picture

Group Events

You can also use groups to announce events. If you're hosting a special promotion or an event that really needs lots of attendees, setting up an event and publicizing it through your Group page definitely gets more attention than the average Facebook

Event invite (see Chapter 11 for details on Facebook Events). An event can promote discussion on the group Wall, which will facilitate interest in the event. Furthermore, people are more apt to attend an event if they see familiar faces going as well. The chances of these faces being familiar are much higher when you're working within the context of a group.

> **FRIENDLY ADVICE**
>
> The group setup makes it much easier to get people involved in what your business is doing. When it comes to united messaging, you can attach files, pictures, and other details. In fact, a Facebook Group may be useful to you not only for external communication, but internal discussions, too. Imagine your employees joining a private Facebook Group where they could discuss issues and concerns. The group messaging makes it even more appealing.

Best Practice on Group Pages

Groups tend to be tighter, more formal, and generally more organized than Fan pages. The trade-off is that they involve more work on your part to make sure everything runs smoothly.

A little chaos is totally understandable on a Fan page, as people can come and go as they please. In a group, you have more control, so you're expected to run a tighter ship. The following sections offer up some general guidelines for keeping your group humming along smoothly.

Connecting Within Groups

Groups are generally smaller than Fan pages, but you still want to make an effort to connect with the individual customers within it.

We recommend gathering a little information about your group members. Facebook gives you a list of all the current people within the group and, depending on their privacy settings, you can glean basic information about each member on his or her Facebook front page. It's less about snooping and more about noticing a pattern. Your vision of the average customer should start to come together—and it may be different than you previously thought.

To get info on group members, click **Members** in the left column underneath the Profile picture. Facebook lists all the members. When you click a member's name, Facebook takes you to that person's personal page.

You can also simply ask members questions as a way to get to know them. Good questions on the Facebook Wall can create a strong, dynamic, and revealing conversation.

> **WATCH OUT**
>
> The hard sell is even more risky on the internet than in the real world. If someone is in your place of business, that means he took the time to come to you, and if he's turned off by a hard sell, he has to find the energy to leave and seek out another provider. On Facebook, a member can leave your group with two clicks of a mouse.

Don't push your business too hard to your group. Doing so can block any potential intimacy you have with your customers. Remember that people Like something or join a group because they love the product and/or they believe in what the company is doing. They already joined your group, so you're at least halfway there. No need for the hard sell. Just treat them with respect.

Remember WIIFM: "What's In It For Me?". You can have the best product or service, but you also have to give your customer incentive to work with you. Make sure you give them more than they need.

Sharing Is Caring

Groups thrive on information and discussion. The source of the information matters less than the information itself. This is why you should take advantage of other people's content.

As an example of what not to do, highly litigious companies like Disney spend millions shutting down homemade projects infringing on their copyrights. Some lawsuits are valid, but most are bullying attempts against people who, at the end of the day, are just really hardcore Disney fans. A five-minute YouTube video of Mickey Mouse made in someone's basement isn't going to hurt Disney's bottom line. The real question is, how big of a Disney fan would you have to be to spend your time and money creating art from its characters?

A wiser decision is to embrace such engagement and creativity from your users, your competition, and even the internet at large. Sharing a funny ad or an art piece can show that it's not about the sale, but about the discussion and sharing that happens within your community. Use discretion and taste when sharing material, but definitely don't turn away the bounty of conversation starters coming from outside of your company.

Get Personal

As a rule, groups are more intimate than Facebook Fan pages, and group members expect to get more personalized treatment.

> **FEEDBACK**
>
> If you have the resources, consider creating a Facebook Fan page or open Group page for the general public and a hidden Group page for your favored customers. You can use the exclusive group to provide perks to customers—for example, telling them about your sales a week before the Facebook Group gets the announcement. The open Facebook Fan or Group page is more appealing to the more casual customer.

Companies often associate the concept of exclusive treatment with spending money, but that's not always the case. Here are some free or low-cost ways to make your customers feel special:

- Post extra photos that didn't make it into the catalog of the latest product.

- Share trivia about your business or products.

- Call out group members and acknowledge them as being loyal customers.

The Least You Need to Know

- Fan pages are open, but Group pages are more exclusive.
- There are three types of Group pages: hidden, closed, and open.
- Groups make it easier to contact all the members directly via email rather than through their News Feed.
- Sharing is paramount in groups, even if it is material from competitors or the members themselves.
- Reward your group members with exclusive peeks into your brand.

Engaging Customers on Facebook

You can get really creative when it comes to getting potential and current customers interested in your Facebook efforts. From viral videos and games to promotions and events, this part gives you the various ways to engage customers. Part 3 also tells you specific ways you can get users to your website and have them engaged enough to stay even after they've completed their purchases.

Harnessing the Power of Friends and Fans

In This Chapter

- Determining how many friends you need
- Understanding the finances of fans
- Harnessing the Facebook News Feed
- The power of losing friends
- Measuring a fan's worth

We've spent some time discussing friends and fans, but what exactly do you *do* with them? It really depends on your business goals. Once those are clear, you can focus on the kind of relationship you'd like your company to have with your potential, current, and life-long customers. In other words, you establish your public persona on Facebook.

In this chapter, we talk about what friends and fans really mean to your business. We also dispel the myth that more friends and fans are always a good thing. News Feeds are like gold to your business, so we discuss how they operate and why a friend or fan's News Feed is an amazing marketing tool.

Friends

When it comes to friends and fans, Facebook is a lot like real life. Facebook friends are people with whom you have a more personal connection, while Facebook fan relationships are more remote, one-way relationships.

Here are some facts about friends:

- Every Facebook user has friends.

- Your actions show up in friends' News Feeds and vice versa.

- Friends can comment on your actions and vice versa.

If you establish your business through a personal Facebook page, you are creating a more casual relationship with your customers.

There are a few situations where a friend-based business could thrive:

- A local small bakery with the same weekly clients

- A town barbershop

- An elementary school

These would work because they all involve relatively intimate relationships and have fewer users. For instance, a small elementary school may have 150 students and 40 employees. Compare their size to an international bank that has 5 million employees and 20 million customers. The bigger the audience, the harder it is to manage the relationships. However, keep in mind that your small business today may become huge tomorrow, so it is often better to create an official business page from the beginning.

WATCH OUT

It's actually much riskier to have friends instead of fans. The intimacy is greater, but so is the vulnerability. For instance, consider if oil giant BP had a friend-based Facebook presence during its catastrophic oil spill in the Gulf of Mexico in 2010. BP's "Friends" would have posted criticism that would have hurt the company more than helped it. The freedom BP's Facebook friends would have to respond, post on its Wall, and other friends-only benefits would have devastated the company—and it already had PR problems with just a Fan page!

Of course, if you're trying to create the next Microsoft or AT&T, the friend route is far too informal. Besides, the larger you get, the harder it is to interact with every customer. And Facebook users expect that kind of intimacy from their friends!

Playing the Numbers Game with Friends

We live in a numbers-driven society. When the stock market is up, everyone's happy. When it goes down, people get a little glum. So it only makes sense that many businesses use the number of fans as a measure of their social marketing success.

The problem is that numbers don't tell the whole story. For instance, your favorite singer could be making a million dollars every time he releases an album, but his credit score could be in the toilet. He could be a millionaire in worse financial shape than the average middle-class American.

Similarly, when it comes to Facebook, there is no "good" number of friends. What matters is the influence you have over them. A high number of friends looks and sounds impressive, but that number won't put money in your business's coffers. The only thing that will sell your service is influence.

Understanding the Power of Friends

Imagine that you're Facebook friends with Bill Gates. Ego aside, there is only one way this will actually matter to your business: if Gates repeats what you say.

Let's run through the process of utilizing Bill Gates' power as a friend:

1. You have to get him to accept your friend request (or you have to accept his).

2. He has to actually pay attention to what your company is posting.

3. He has to find your post compelling enough to share with his friends.

Without the final step, your friendship with Gates means nothing to your business. Instead of focusing on the number of friends, you should focus on drawing in powerful, influential friends. Both authors of this book, John and Damon, have many, many Facebook friends, but some of their most valuable Facebook moments were when a major tastemaker mentioned them in a Facebook post or gave them praise on their Facebook Wall.

Damon remembers one heavy hitter giving one of his books a glowing review on his Facebook Wall—and it caused enough of a stir to create a buzz and drum up sales.

FRIENDLY ADVICE

Remember that Facebook friendships are about intimacy, not the sale. If you keep your interactions personal, you'll get the sale as well as the relationship.

Adding and Deleting Friends

Longtime Facebookers go through a regular process we like to call *pruning:* dropping inactive friends, removing themselves from boring or annoying groups, and so on. Think of it as a form of spring cleaning.

DEFINITION

Pruning on Facebook is the process of deleting any friends, groups, and memberships you don't want anymore.

As a business, you should also do regular pruning. Why lose a potential customer? There are actually several reasons, including these:

- They post inappropriate messages on your company Wall.

- They post an excessive number of messages on your company Wall.

- They haven't taken any actions in a long time.

- For whatever reason, they are of no value to your business.

WATCH OUT

Pruning should be a slow and methodical process, especially if you are removing someone because you don't think he or she will be useful in the future. Nearly everyone knows someone who can use your service, so be careful dismissing someone too early. She may have a second cousin who could really use your product!

A friend who isn't engaged isn't a friend at all. He or she is just another digit in your friend total. It sounds counterintuitive to dump friends, but your main goal should be to replace that bum friend with an active friend. Back to the Bill Gates example, the Microsoft founder is just one friend, but he carries the power of thousands.

Here are some tips for approaching new potential friends for your business:

- **Craft a finely worded introduction.** Facebook doesn't require you to write an intro, but it's a key component to your marketing approach.

- **Have a clear Profile picture.** Like we talked about earlier in the book, your Profile picture is likely the only thing a potential customer sees before he or she decides to join or not join your page.

- **Be patient.** Some people take months to respond to Facebook friend requests, but a late response doesn't mean that they're ignoring you.

- **Don't spam your customers.** Make sure you know the people you invite on some kind of personal level. If you continuously invite people you don't know, you can end up in Facebook jail where they prevent you from any more friend invites.

FEEDBACK

When choosing between friends and fans, remember that your friends actually have to accept your Facebook request. Some people rarely check their friend requests, while others let them pile up and add them only a few times a year—kind of like the reverse of pruning. Either way, you could spend much more time finding friends and waiting for acceptance than building your business.

Fans

The term "fans" is one of the biggest misnomers in Facebook. Conjures up images of Justin Bieber–singing teenagers, doesn't it? The funny name probably came about because Fan pages were originally built for musicians, actors, and other celebrities. As Facebook expanded, it realized that companies were interested in Fan pages, too.

Understanding the Power of Fans

If friends are the one-on-one conversation, fans are the megaphone to the masses.

Here are some facts about fans:

- Individuals can't have fans unless they create a Fan page.
- Your actions show up in your fans' News Feeds, but your fans' actions don't show up in yours.
- Fans can comment on your page.

FEEDBACK

If you want anyone to comment on your page, not just fans, then go to the Options menu and you can choose who can post on your fan Wall, with options ranging from "anyone," "fans," and "no one."

Unlike friend-based pages, with a Fan page you can connect with your customers with more control over what is posted on your page.

Fan-based business pages are much more common for businesses, especially among larger, more corporate businesses such as the following:

- A chamber of commerce

- A Fortune 500 company

- A large law firm

They tend to be more formal and focused more on getting a particular message or piece of knowledge out rather than having one-on-one conversations with customers.

Calculating a Fan's Worth

When it comes to determining a fan's worth, the argument is as heated as religion and politics. Estimates vary widely, with three different companies specializing in this kind of thing estimating the worth at anywhere from $3.60 to $136.80 per fan. The disparity is pretty amusing—unless you're the one in charge of the marketing budget.

The amount you want to spend on getting additional fans really depends on your business. If you are selling $2 ice cream cones, the amount you're willing to spend is probably much lower than if you sell luxury goods.

FRIENDLY ADVICE

Facebook launched its new feature, Timeline, in late 2011. It gives you a visual representation of your history on Facebook.

How can it be valuable to your business? It actually tracks all the events that have happened on your Facebook page—including when people unfriended you, stopped liking your page, and other details. Much of this information has been available to you already, as we will discuss in Chapter 16 on analytics, but with Timeline, Facebook has made tracking your daily, monthly, and even yearly changes more user-friendly.

For more information on Timeline, go to www.facebook.com/about/timeline.

It also depends on how you make your money. Think about Zynga, the über-popular social gaming company behind FarmVille and Mafia Wars. Zynga makes its money on ads as well as small in-game purchases. Getting another fan increases the number of people viewing the ads, and the more viewers it has, the more money it can charge for its ads.

> **FRIENDLY ADVICE**
>
> The Zynga business model totally transformed how companies market their business and make a profit on Facebook. See Chapter 13 for more on games.

Follow these steps to figure out how much you should spend per fan:

1. Figure out how much the average customer spends during the course of his or her relationship with your business.

2. Determine how many customers are being referred to you through Facebook.

3. Weigh in other social and traditional media, comparing the price per new customer to the cost of Facebook customers.

4. Decide what portion of your marketing budget Facebook merits.

Scaling Walls and News Feeds

Walls and News Feeds sound like a variant of the childhood game Chutes and Ladders, but it's actually the best way to communicate with your audience on Facebook.

The Anatomy of a Wall

Let's check out your Wall:

- Go to www.facebook.com.

- Log in.

- Click your name in the upper-right corner.

All the information below your Profile is your Facebook Wall (see Figure 9.1). It is essentially a listing of all your actions as well as anything friends have said about you.

Figure 9.1: *A Facebook Wall.*

Walls are important, but *News Feeds* are your best bet to communicate. A person's News Feed tells him what's happening on Facebook right now.

DEFINITION

A **News Feed** is a chronological listing of every action your friends and Fan pages have taken on Facebook. It automatically updates by default, even if you don't refresh the page.

Let's go deeper into how News Feeds operate and how you can take advantage of them.

The Anatomy of a News Feed

The News Feed is the first thing people see when they log in to Facebook. In fact, many people probably view their News Feed more than their own Profile page Wall. While your Wall shows everything related to you, the broader News Feed shows you what everyone else is doing. And isn't that the main reason why people go on Facebook?

As of Fall 2011, the Facebook News Feed has two parts:

- **Most Recent:** Shows the latest actions from all the people and organizations that you follow. If your Aunt Betsy just updated her relationship status, you'll see it here the moment it happens.

- **Top Stories:** Facebook focuses its News Feed on the people you interact with the most.

Facebook organizes the News Feed by Top Stories by default. To organize your News Feed by Most Recent items, click the link at the top of the screen.

Believe it or not, most recent updates used to be the only option for News Feeds. The problem is that everyone follows some people or businesses that they don't really care about. For instance, finding out what your best friend is up to is probably more important than hearing what your classmate from high school had for dinner last night. In other words, News Feed originally had no way of prioritizing information.

FRIENDLY ADVICE

In late 2011, Facebook added Subscriptions, another way users can follow your latest news. Subscriptions are for individual pages, so you can technically have the audience created with a Fan or Group page on your personal page without having to become friends with every person connected to you. We appreciate the option, but we still recommend creating a unique Fan or Group page instead of just directing people to your personal page. Always opt to take the more professional route.

To subscribe to someone, click the **Subscribe** icon in the left column underneath an individual's Profile picture.

Top Stories came about as a response to Twitter. If you are familiar with Twitter, you know that there is no way to prioritize information on that site: messages get pushed down as more recent posts appear. Facebook decided it needed an edge over the service, and so it created the Top Stories option.

Now Facebook prioritizes your News Feed based on two things:

- The topics being discussed the most among your friends
- The people you interact with the most

Regarding the first way, Facebook tries to decide what topics are trending among your friends and makes them a priority on your News Feed. For example, if 20 of your friends have posted something related to, say, the 2012 U.S. Presidential election, Facebook puts those posts at the top of your News Feed.

Second, Facebook observes who you communicate with the most and gives their posts high priority on your News Feed. These are the people, Fan pages, or businesses that you do Wall posts on, share content with, or Like. Facebook uses an algorithm to determine the most important ones in your Facebook life.

Top Stories is good news in that once you get an engaged customer, your news is more likely to get priority in her Feed. The bad news is that with other people and companies vying for your fans' attention, it's more difficult to actually get into their Feed, and so the customer won't see what's going on with you unless she visits your Wall.

Getting into Friends' and Fans' Top Stories

The goal, of course, is to get into and stay within a customer's Top Stories. Here are some tips for staying on the radar.

- **Update your content often.** The more you update, the higher the chances are that they will actually see you on their News Feed.

- **Mention Facebook users by name.** If it's appropriate for your business, feel free to "shout out" a favorite customer. The mention not only puts you in his Top Stories section but also automatically places you on his Wall.

- **Give incentives for mentioning your products and services.** We recommend coming up with several incentives to get your fans to mention you. One idea that takes little effort is showcasing a "fan of the week."

- **Encourage users who visit your Fan page to Like you right away.** As we mentioned earlier, a Like automatically prioritizes that person's interest in your company. Likes also appear on friends' News Feeds, and they may be curious enough to learn more about your product.

- **Push a conversation.** Everyone loves giving an opinion on Facebook. Even if you don't get the answers you expect, any stimulating conversations add more comments and Likes to your post. The more responses, the higher the post will get prioritized in everyone's News Feed.

- **Use media such as photos and videos.** These get a higher chance of appearing in the Feed than text-only posts.

The Least You Need to Know

- A Facebook friend typically represents a personal relationship, while a Facebook fan represents a more professional relationship.
- One or two influential friends or fans are way more important than 100 docile, unengaged parties.
- A Wall shows a person's actions. A News Feed shows the action of the person's friends and Fan pages.
- The Top Stories in News Feeds are those posted by multiple friends or by the friends you interact with the most.

Social Media Engagement

In This Chapter

- Figuring out why users like your Fan page
- Encouraging continual engagement
- Establishing a strong brand presence
- Using promotion to drive traffic to your page
- Adding social plugins to your Facebook site

Social media is all about interaction. You create a Facebook account and set up a Fan page or group for your business for the single-minded purpose of engaging with your customers. That interaction can take many forms—from someone clicking the **Like** icon to posting a comment on your site.

Things That Make Them Like Your Business

To have a successful Facebook presence, you first need to ask one question: Why in the world would anyone want to Like your business on Facebook when there are millions of other great pages?

People choose to Like Facebook pages for a wide variety of reasons, but at the end of the day, it all comes down to positive relationships.

Unless you reach out to the people in a business, you never really develop a true liking that sticks. People are the piece that keeps you coming back for more.

You want people to reach out to your business, so you have to spark conversations that get them to interact with you.

FEEDBACK

Think for a moment of a business that you like (outside of Facebook) and why you like it. Co-author John is a big fan of his chiropractors, Drs. Seema and Arun Mani in Geneva, Illinois. John doesn't just like the services his chiropractors perform, but the conversations he has every time he sees them. They connect. They have a relationship. John knows where each doctor went for vacation on spring break and what their favorite part of the trip was. They, in turn, know that his family went swimming at the local water park and had a blast. Replicate the same relationship on Facebook. Get personal.

The Top Five Ways to Engage Your Fans

You should post news on your Facebook Wall on a weekly basis. Some fans will comment on your posts and some won't. Don't discount the individuals who don't post on your Wall. You've got to give people time to warm up. And some posts will resonate with some people and not others. Here are some suggestions for getting more engagement your fans:

Use action words. When you first start winning fans, you will get engagement simply by asking for it. Use action words like *Visit, Click, Share, Post, Like, Watch,* and *Tell Us* ….

Action words motivate fans to engage. They help make your message stand out from among the thousands of messages people see each day.

Keep your posts short. The many studies done on Facebook engagement reveal that the shorter the posts, the more people engage with them.

To maximize engagement, try to limit your Facebook posts to no more than 85 characters. (About the length of the previous sentence!)

Post when people are on Facebook. Most people engage on Facebook during the morning before work (7 A.M.), right after work (5 P.M.), and late at night (11 P.M.). If you can reach them when they're online, you have a better chance of getting them to speak their mind.

Make them laugh out loud. People love to laugh. Posting funny thoughts brings out the best in people and gets them talking. If you can get people to laugh, you've got engagement.

Ask questions. When someone asks you a question, you instinctively want to answer it. That's why questions work well on Facebook. Ask away: *Who? What? When? Where? How?*

> **WATCH OUT**
>
> Try to avoid asking "Why" questions. These can be seen as invasive and fans tend to shy away from them.

Imprinting Your Brand

Your brand is one of the most important assets of your business on Facebook. We're not talking about logos and tag lines, but what these stand for: what your business does, how you're different from your competition, and why customers should buy from you.

These are the kinds of things you need to instill in your fans. Brands imprint emotions. People see brands and have instant opinions of them. For example, Martha Stewart's brand isn't about homemaking per se, but about taking the painstaking time to create a wonderful home. When you use one of Martha's products, it shows to yourself and to others that you are emotionally invested in making the best living space possible. What emotional reaction do you want customers to have when they think of your brand?

Here are some brands on Facebook you might not be familiar with. Notice how they establish their brand and what they offer their fans. What is likable about them?

Dog Bless You (www.facebook.com/exploredogs). A brand dedicated to championing the selfless acts of others. Their Fan page shares stories of owners and their dogs.

For every 5,000 Likes, they gift a dog to a soldier living with PTSD.

American Association of Medical Assistants. A brand dedicated to passionately serving medical-assisting professionals through education, certification, and networking.

Liking their page (see Figure 10.1) gets you access to exclusive Facebook content such as their posts, contests, and exclusive talks with their leaders. Another key feature of this site is that it enables members to "connect with colleagues."

Figure 10.1: *The American Association of Medical Assistants Facebook page.*

Puritan Cleaners (see Figure 10.2). A brand dedicated to not only local dry cleaning in Richmond, Virginia, but to serving the community at large through charitable events. This is the most active dry cleaner in the country when it comes to social media and Facebook marketing. They change their Fan page often with the charitable events they cover.

Like their page and see why they have been selected as one of America's Best Cleaners.

Figure 10.2: *The Puritan Cleaners Facebook page.*

Chick-fil-A (www.facebook.com/ChickfilA). A brand dedicated to serving great food and establishing community connections. Like their page and see why their fans love them.

You want people to see your brand on Facebook and the first thing that pops into their mind is, "These guys are the best and that's why I am a fan."

How you craft your message represents your brand on Facebook.

> **FRIENDLY ADVICE**
>
> Give visitors reasons to Like you on your Facebook Fan page, such as "We like you. So here are a few reasons to like us …" or "Like us to get access to discounts to some of the best restaurants in your local area."

What Keeps Them Coming Back

People revisit Fan and Group pages because they're looking for the latest news, the greatest tips, and because they want to be entertained and feel good. You're not going to fill these needs if you only post once a month. Instead, you should plan to update your page weekly or daily.

What you post is as important as how frequently you post. Here are suggestions for postings that will encourage people to check out your site regularly:

- Write snappy Wall posts about current events.

- Use large vertical images, which tend to stand out on the Facebook Wall.

- Use videos in Wall posts. Videos stick out of the crowd because they're highly engaging. The large blue button on the image of the video also stands out.

> **FEEDBACK**
>
> You have to start somewhere with engagement. Reach out to your loyal customers and ask them to help you by commenting on a regular basis. Priming the pump with comments gets the conversations started, and frequent updates keep them going.

Promotions Drive Traffic and Fans

Contests and sweepstakes are very effective means of driving traffic to Facebook Fan pages. However, Facebook has very strict rules for using Fan pages to conduct promotions.

Drive Traffic with Contests and Sweepstakes

Contests and promotions are a solid way to bring interest, traffic, and ideally loyalty to your brand. Contests can be as simple as giving a free product randomly to a user who Likes your Facebook page this month. Promotions can be a limited sale, a new product line, or any major marketing push exclusive for the moment.

Companies can easily use third-party tools to create contests and promotions. For instance, the Sell Fine Art Facebook website (see Figure 10.3) has its promotion built right into its Facebook page.

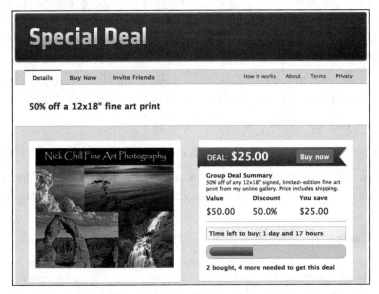

Figure 10.3: *The Sell Fine Art Facebook website.*

FEEDBACK

Wildfire is a third-party app provider that enables users to run 10 different types of promotions, including sweepstakes, group deals, photo/design contests, video contests, essay contests, quizzes, and trivia. They can be found at www. wildfireapp.com.

A few great app resources for contests, sweepstakes, polls, and more are as follows:

- Involver (www.involver.com)
- Votigo (vwww.votigo.com)
- Strutta (www.strutta.com)
- EasyPromos (www.easypromosapp.com)
- Offerpop (www.offerpop.com)
- Fanappz (www.fanappz.com)

The Rules

Facebook has some very strict rules for running promotions on Facebook. In a nutshell, they are:

- You can't use Facebook's features/tools for the promotions. This includes getting users to Like posts, videos, or images. The Like button is not a voting tool and cannot be used as one.

- Promotions must be administered through a third-party application on an app on a page tab or canvas page.

- You can't use Facebook messaging—this includes chat, email, posts, and messages—to notify winners.

- You can't use the Facebook name or trademarks except as needed to hold Facebook blameless. You must include a disclaimer saying that Facebook is in no way associated with the promotion; all entrants release Facebook of any such claim; and all data is going to the Fan page owner, not to Facebook.

FRIENDLY ADVICE

Here's some sample language to use in your disclaimer: <Your PageName> does not endorse, sponsor, or administer this promotion. This promotion is in no way sponsored, endorsed, or administered by or associated with Facebook. By participating, you hereby release and hold harmless Facebook from any and all liability associated with this promotion.

Facebook's legal rules can change at a moment's notice, so go to www.facebook.com to read the latest guidelines.

Promotions FAQs

People don't always read the finer details of contest rules and inadvertently break a rule. Here are some frequently asked questions about running promotions on Facebook:

Can you have a drawing and select a random fan and give them a prize?

According to the rules, it's a big fat *no*. Why? Because you're using Facebook's tools to do this.

How can I inform a winner that he or she won?

You aren't allowed to email/comment/post on their Wall/chat to the winners from within Facebook to tell them they won. You have to make sure to collect their email and use your non-Facebook email to message them. Smoke signals work, too.

Can I get them to Like my page, and then present them with a contest?

Sure. You can get them to Like a page, check in, or use your app. But you may not use anything beyond these three things. (We discuss check-ins more in Chapter 18.)

WATCH OUT

If you run a contest on Facebook without using a third-party service, it is probably against the rules and you could get banned. For example, you can't use the simple act of a person Liking a page or checking in to a place to automatically register him or her for a promotion.

Check out the complete guidelines online at www.facebook.com/promotions_guidelines.php.

Facebook Social Plugins

Keep in mind that once someone becomes a fan, he will see your posts on his Wall. Unless, that is, he decides that his Feed is too cluttered with your posts and he hides your feed or Unlikes you.

If he hides you, you keep the fan count but lose his attention. This is worse than his Unliking you. At least then you would not be talking to air.

In order to avoid having fans tune you out, you need to keep them engaged. Within your Fan page on Facebook, there is a section called Resources (see Figure 10.4). This section has tools that let you see what your friends have Liked, commented on, or shared on sites across the internet.

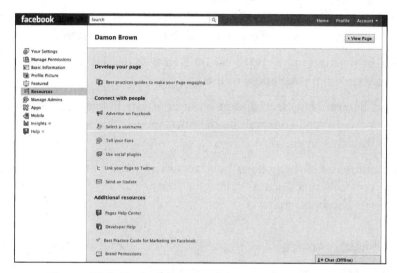

Figure 10.4: *Facebook Resources help you get even more social.*

To get to your resources follow these steps:

1. Go to your business page.

2. Click **See All** in the upper-right corner.

3. Click **Resources** in the right column.

These *plugins* give you an opportunity to reach fans outside of Facebook when they visit your website.

DEFINITION

A **plugin** is a piece of software that changes the behavior of a website.

Social Buttons

The following plugins give you an opportunity to reach fans outside of Facebook when they visit your Facebook website.

The Like Button. The Like button lets fans share pages from your website back to their Facebook Profile. When the fan clicks the **Like** button on your site, a post appears in her friends' News Feed with a link back to your website.

This is a highly engaging tactic to use on your website. Try to keep this button near the top of your site if you choose to use it.

The Send Button. The Send button shoots a private note to a fan's friends. Fans have the option to send your website in a message to their Facebook friends, to a group Wall, and as an email.

This is reminiscent of the popular Send to a Friend option that used to appear on websites. This new functionality takes the sharing to a new level by automatically opening your Facebook contacts.

> **FRIENDLY ADVICE**
>
> Combinations work well. If you want to use both the Send and Like button on your website, you can access a combined version of them from the Resources link.

Login Button. The Login button enables Facebook users to sign in to Facebook from your website. The plugin also shows pictures of your fan's friends who have already fanned or friended your Facebook page.

The Login button grabs users' attention on your website and sends the message that your business is forward-thinking and integrated with Facebook. It also shows them actual fans. Social proof says it all.

Social Activity

Social activity plugins make it easier for customers to comment, post, or otherwise interact with your Facebook page. They also allow deeper interactions, like registering for lists and suggestions for your related pages.

Comments. The Facebook Comments plugin enables Facebook users to comment on content on your website. It even has a personalized moderation/distribution option. When a user engages in the Comments Box on your site, a post appears in her friends' News Feed with a link back to your site.

Activity Feed. The Activity Feed plugin shows users what their friends are doing on your website. It displays the most recent activity on your site, such as when users Like content from your site, share content from your site in Facebook, or comment in a Facebook Comments Box on your site.

When a user is logged in to Facebook, the plugin highlights content from their friends. If the user isn't logged in to Facebook, the Feed shows recommendations from your site and gives the user the option to log in to Facebook via a link on the Feed. This is a powerful plugin that pulls in a lot of activity from Facebook to your website.

Recommendations. The Recommendations plugin gives your website users suggestions for pages on your site they might like. It works by looking at all the social interactions from your site. A user who is logged in to Facebook sees pages his or her friends have engaged on.

Think of this as a "you might also be interested in" feature to get users to visit all the popular areas of your website.

Registration. The Registration plugin enables users to log in to your website with their Facebook account. When users are logged in to Facebook already, they are presented with a form that is pre-filled with their Facebook information.

This is a great way to pre-fill in as much information as possible on a form on your website. It's a usability factor that makes your checkout process for e-commerce that much easier for your customers.

Social Streams

Social streams compile all your Facebook activity into an easier-to-navigate page. You can use them to quickly assess who is on your Facebook page and how to reach them more effectively.

Facepile. The Facepile plugin displays the Facebook Profile pictures of users who have Liked your page or have signed up for your site. It's a simple tool to show the users the faces that support your business.

Like Box. The Like box enables users to Like your Facebook page and view its stream from your website.

This is a great way to get people to Like your Fan page from your website. This is similar to Facepile, with some added options for showing a stream and header. It's a matter of personal preference in design as to which one you use. The one-click feature to become a fan is the greatest value of this tool.

Live Stream. The Live Stream plugin lets users share Facebook activity and comments in real time as they interact during a live event.

As businesses are conducting more meetings online, this plugin is likely to grow in popularity. It's an excellent tool for live streaming video in e-meetings such as webcasts and webinars.

The Least You Need to Know

- Keep your Facebook posts short. The shorter the posts, the more engagement.
- Most people engage on Facebook before work (7 A.M.), right after work (5 P.M.), and late at night (11 P.M.). That's when you should plan to engage with them.
- Always use a third-party service to run a contest or promotion on Facebook. If you violate Facebook's rules on promotions, you could be banned from the site.
- Facebook plugins give you an opportunity to reach fans outside of Facebook when they visit your website.

Facebook Events and Pictures

In This Chapter

- Creating Facebook Events
- Using RSVPs wisely
- Knowing whom to invite
- Tagging pictures and using them as marketing tools

Facebook isn't all about connecting with people via the Wall, News Feed, and messages. Depending on your business, you want your customers to support you by actually physically showing up somewhere. For instance, if you own a restaurant, you can't just thrive on virtual connections—instead, you want people to show up to eat at your place of business.

In this chapter, we talk about the art of the invitation, whether it is RSVPing tastemakers in your business, using video to entice customers, or respectfully using picture-tagging to get attention. We also show you what not to do.

Facebook Events

Facebook is so successful in part because it bridges two worlds:

- People's real lives
- People's virtual lives

Facebook Events are powerful because they give your business the opportunity to turn a virtual friend or fan into a real-life, paying customer.

Events are also relatively easy to set up: after you get the hang of it, you'll be creating new events in a matter of minutes. The danger, of course, is that the simplicity makes it easy to throw together an event without much planning or forethought. You need to think them through as carefully as one you would design through an event planner.

Types of Events

You can launch three types of major events using Facebook:

- A visit
- A purchase
- A conversation

The following sections explore each of these event types in detail.

The Visit Event

A visit is anything that requires the invitee to get up from the computer chair and head somewhere. However, Facebook still tends to be easier to execute than a mass-mailing campaign or other multimedia approach. In fact, in certain circumstances, it is virtually your only option. For instance, if you're holding a last-minute in-store sale, you don't have time to do a magazine ad or maybe not even a newspaper or radio ad. Sending a note through your email list may work, but just as often emails get caught in spam filters—or they get through the filters but people don't bother to read them. Over half of Facebook's 800 million users visit the site at least once a day, so chances are high that they will see your event.

FRIENDLY ADVICE

A good example of a visit would be Damon's book tour for his critically acclaimed book *Porn & Pong: How Grand Theft Auto, Tomb Raider and Other Sexy Games Changed Our Culture.* Released through the indie publisher Feral House, the book had a nice buzz before it was released but had little to no advertising budget.

Damon took it into his own hands and organized a cross-country tour entirely through email, Twitter, LinkedIn, and Facebook. From Chicago book signings to Las Vegas speaking engagements, Facebook Events would keep his fans up on where he would be next. The Facebook price (free!) and easy event-making made it possible for him to have a very successful tour while still maintaining his business—and without the money or the frustration that usually come with it.

You can organize a wide variety of types of visits, including the following:

- Concerts

- In-store sales

- Seminars

- Movie premieres

The Purchase Event

A purchase is anything that asks the invitee to buy something remotely—usually an online purchase, but it could apply to ordering over the phone or even via the mail.

For instance, your favorite musician could have an event for her new album's launch day. By observing how many people are attending the event—or how many people say no to the event!—the artist can get a better idea about her upcoming sales. It also would be beneficial for the artist to promote sales that day, because those first-week sales determine how high the album will reach on the charts.

Here are some purchase examples:

- Album releases

- Online sales

- Book launches

The Conversation Event

A conversation involves asking users to discuss or support a particular agenda.

For example, a charity might ask supporters to change their Facebook Profile picture to its logo for a day in support of its cause. It's a free gesture for the participant, and, for that day, the charity gets its fans to show a united front on Facebook.

Here are some other examples of conversations:

- Petitions

- Online discussions

- Virtual classes

- Live podcasts

Creating Your First Event

To create an event on Facebook, log in to Facebook, click **Events** in the left column, and click **Create an Event** at the top of the screen.

On the Create an Event screen (see Figure 11.1), fill in the following details:

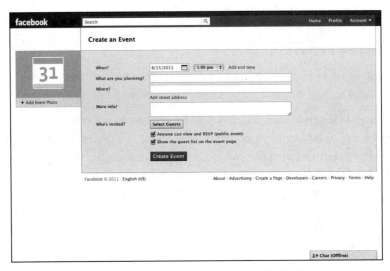

Figure 11.1: *Creating an event on Facebook.*

- **Event picture:** To add an event picture, click **Add Event Photo** and upload a photo from your computer (see Figure 11.2).

Figure 11.2: *Choosing a picture for your Facebook Event.*

FRIENDLY ADVICE

The event picture is crucial—don't even think about creating an event without including one! If you're not sure what to use, consider these options:

- Your company logo
- A picture of your product
- A happy customer

If you don't include an event picture, Facebook will give your event a generic date icon. Facebook is, first and foremost, a visual medium. Like your Profile page, your event page will probably be judged solely by its picture. If no picture exists, people probably won't click on it.

- **Date:** Indicate the day, month, and year of the event.

- **Begin and, if applicable, end time:** Event planners are doing really interesting things with the begin and end times. For instance, some promotions don't set an end date and use the event Wall as a de-facto message board. We recommend a more standard method through a Facebook page, but some organizations are making it work.

- **Name of Event:** Keep it short and snappy. Think about it like a newspaper headline or a very brief tweet. Like all marketing, the following keywords work great in an event name:

  - Free

  - Exclusive

  - Limited

  - Trial

  - NEW!

  - Food

- **Location and, if applicable, street address:** If you do have a location for your event, be sure to fill out the complete address. When you launch your event page, Facebook will provide a map link so visitors can plan their trip.

- **Additional info/description:** Limit your description of the event to two short paragraphs—the first one for your event and the second one for your business bio.

- **Selected guests:** Selecting your guests can be the most time-consuming part of the process. Even if you have an "open" event where everyone can come, you still want to personally invite people you definitely want to come. Sending a brief invitation can make the difference between someone showing up to support you and someone not bothering to come.

> **FEEDBACK**
>
> Short attention spans aside, there's another reason why you want to keep your event descriptions short: Facebook actually cuts them off.
>
> Your event page only shows a few lines of description, but to read any additional text, users must click **See More**. If you haven't caught their attention in the beginning, your potential clients aren't going to ask for more.

- **RSVP and guest-list settings:** You have two yes-or-no choices:

  - Anyone can view or RSVP (public event).

  - Show the guest list on the event page.

If you choose Yes for the first option, then you are making it a public event, and it will …

  - Show up on attendees' Walls—and therefore their friends' News Feeds.

  - Allow anyone to RSVP.

  - Give details about your affair to people not connected to you or your guests.

On the other hand, private events …

  - Don't show up on attendees' Walls.

  - Only allow invitees to RSVP.

  - Won't show up when searched for by people who are not invited to the event.

Showing the guest list also depends largely on the type of event you'd like to have. There are many reasons to hide or show the guest list.

Presenting the guest list can …

- Encourage people to join if their friends are coming.

- Show off the movers and shakers attending your event.

- Let people know how big your event is going to be.

Hiding the guest list is equally powerful, as it can …

- Prevent people from knowing if someone they don't like is coming.

- Keep the privacy of those attending.

- Enable you to make the event seem much bigger than it actually is.

> **FRIENDLY ADVICE**
>
> Every good club promoter knows that most RSVPs happen within 24 hours of the event. One party promoter told Damon that he expects RSVPs to double the day of the event. If you need a big turnout to impress people, be careful with making your RSVP list public. People on the fence about coming to your event may see the early RSVP list—when it is still paltry—and decide not to come.

You're finally ready to create your event! Click **Create Event** and your event displays.

Getting Influencers to Attend Your Event

Influencers, or the tastemakers that can make or break your product, are the very reason why you have events. You want them to come, be impressed, and tell everyone else about it. People trust influencers, so if they speak highly of you, they will trust you, too.

Determining who an influencer is really depends on your business, and you're the best expert when it comes to deciding who they are and how to get them to attend.

However, keep the following general guidelines in mind when trying to get an influencer to your event:

- Approach him or her in an original way.

- Avoid nagging or spamming.

- Focus on making a good impression.

- Assume that you're making a relationship beyond the event.
- Try to make his or her social circle interested in the event.

The last point about the influencer's social circle is worth discussing. Think about it this way: if a nice stranger on the street told you to attend a cool party, chances are that you'd be more than skeptical. However, if your friends told you about that same cool party, you'd consider going.

A person's social circle has more power than any you can ever hope to have as a company. Find out who the influencer hangs out with and see if there's another way to get closer to him.

Using Facebook Pictures to Connect with Customers

Pictures are the lifeblood of Facebook. When someone gets married, when she buys a new car, or when she goes on an adventure, she posts pictures on Facebook.

Facebook pics give you the rare opportunity to connect with users on an intimate level without having to do a friend request, encourage Likes, or spam them.

People Love Pictures of Themselves

One of the reasons why people love Facebook is that they get a chance to see themselves. Their friends, family, and colleagues are great, but it's more about how these important people relate to the user. It's not just about seeing what your relative is doing, but also how importantly they view you.

A good marketing strategy is to tap into users' own egotism and make them feel like a star. For instance, years ago, Captain Morgan rum began an ad campaign hyping up the Captain Morgan pose: lifting your leg up so your knee touched your elbow. The memorable pose had a small advertising buzz, but then Captain Morgan distiller Diageo decided to open a contest to the public. The Captain Morgan Pose Off rewarded customers who took pictures of their best pose. It ended up being a huge success, especially after the company started uploading the pictures to Facebook. A customer would see his picture on the Captain Morgan Facebook page and, naturally, share it with his friends.

Marketing via Tagging

Tagging is traditionally done to identify a person in a picture, but you can also use it to communicate with people. You can tag anyone on Facebook (see Figure 11.3).

> **DEFINITION**
>
> **Tagging** is the process of putting someone's name in a Facebook picture. Facebook notifies the individual when they are tagged, so some businesses use it as a marketing tool to get people's attention.

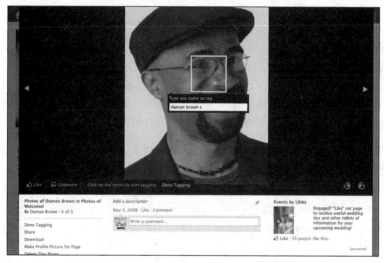

Figure 11.3: *Tagging a picture on Facebook.*

Creating a Tag

Here's how you tag a picture:

1. Upload the picture you want to tag.

2. Open the picture in Facebook.

3. Click **Tag This Picture** in the lower-left corner of the screen.

4. Click on the area of the picture where you'd like the person tagged.

5. Type his or her name.

6. Press the **Enter** key to confirm. Facebook sends an email notice to the person along with a direct link to the picture.

If you made a mistake, you can delete the tag by clicking on the tagged area and pressing the **Delete** key.

> **WATCH OUT**
>
> Facebook sends individuals a message immediately after you tag them, whether you delete it later or not. Be careful, as tagging the wrong people could make them pretty upset—even if you fix it later!

This works as a marketing tool for a couple reasons. First, when you tag someone in a picture, Facebook sends the person a notice. Out of curiosity, he or she will more than likely go to the picture and check it out. Second, it puts you in the driver's seat. The image could be anything—your latest product or a flyer for an upcoming event. It's like an advertisement that reaches out to customers.

Marketing via tagging is also pretty limited. To tag someone, you must, of course, know her name. Figuring out names takes resources.

Most importantly, tagging can quickly turn into aggressive spamming. When you think about it, the parallels are pretty obvious: sending unsolicited messages to an individual with the hopes that he'll click on a link and come to your page.

> **WATCH OUT**
>
> Your reputation can be destroyed quickly if you become an overzealous tagger. Damon was tagged in one photo that had nothing to do with what he was interested in, showing that the person hadn't done his research, and, additionally, tagged him along with it seemed like 100 other people. It was impersonal in the very worst way, and Damon dropped his association with the Facebook colleague shortly afterward.

If you do decide to tag, keep a few things in mind:

- It's better to tag a few key people than to tag dozens of folks in one photo.

- Make sure your message is clear in the photo.

- In general, don't tag a person more than once or twice.

The Least You Need to Know

- Facebook Events can involve a visit, a purchase, or a conversation.
- You can create an event free of charge in only a few minutes.
- Facebook Events can be private or public affairs.
- Tagging people in pictures is a quick way to get attention, but it should be used sparingly as a marketing tool.

Viral Videos

In This Chapter

- Making cool content
- Knowing what will be passed along
- Understanding sticky entertainment
- Getting a grip on edutainment
- Touring the Facebook toolbox

You've probably heard a lot references to *viral marketing* these days. Viral videos and viral ads seem to be all the rage. But what exactly does it all mean? When it comes to viral marketing, it means a brand that has an ad or promotion that people like so much they share it with their friends.

Although viral marketing is a relatively new term, the concept has been around for a long time. Think about the "Where's the beef?" ads the fast-food giant Wendy's ran in the mid-'80s, or the "Plop plop fizz fizz" associated with Alka Seltzer for decades.

So why is everyone talking about viral now and not back then? The answer is in large part due to the internet and social networking sites like Facebook. This means that your business has more power to make a social impact than at any other time in history.

Facebook Video

Text and pictures are cool, but the next big thing in Facebook is video. In fact, it's less about Facebook and more a reflection of our craving for more videos online. We can thank faster internet connections and the success of YouTube for that.

Pictures are still the main way marketers are communicating on Facebook, so anything you can do with video will be both original and memorable.

So why doesn't everyone do video? Here are some reasons:

- A well-done video can be exponentially more expensive than a well-done photo.
- Businesses can be intimidated by the prospect of recording video.
- Text or even pictures are faster and easier to create than video.

FRIENDLY ADVICE

A low-end video may actually fit your style. If you're promoting a hipster bar in New York, for example, you really don't want an overly polished product. Use your audience's expectations to set your budget and goals.

In other words, creating a video is quite an endeavor. The rewards are just as great as the risks, though.

Uploading Videos

You have three primary ways to get videos into your customer's hands:

- Your Facebook page
- Your Facebook messaging
- Your customer's Wall

The following sections explore each of these options in detail.

Uploading to Your Facebook Page

To upload a video, log in to Facebook and go to your company Profile page. Click **Video** at the top of the Wall (see Figure 12.1).

Figure 12.1: *Adding video to your Facebook page.*

Choose one of the following options:

- Record a video with a webcam.

- Upload a video from your drive.

The first option is fine if you want to create a short, casual message. It will be super-casual, though, so we recommend knowing your audience very well before taking that route. You'll need a webcam-enabled computer. Some computers, like the higher-end Macs, have a built-in webcam, but you can also buy a decent webcam for less than $100 that you can plug in to your USB outlet.

When you're ready, click on the link and Facebook will begin recording through your webcam.

Uploading your video from your drive is a much safer and, perhaps, wiser choice. With this option, you record the video with a digital recorder, edit it as you see fit, and then upload the file straight from your computer.

WATCH OUT

People are sometimes compelled to record directly onto Facebook to keep the casual look, but the same feel can be done using a handheld device or even a webcam recording onto your computer instead of onto Facebook. You then have the ability to edit or scrap the video instead of having the pressure to post it after you record it on the website.

When you upload a video to your Facebook page, a link appears in the News Feed of people who already Like your Facebook page. People who visit your Facebook page will easily be able to share it with others.

Sending Video as a Message

You can also send out the video as an attachment to a Facebook message. This way works with Facebook Groups (see Chapter 8).

Your group members receive the email at the same time, and they can view the video within Facebook—even if it's a YouTube-based recording. This works particularly well for infrequent Facebook users. Facebook gives them a notification in their regular email with the Facebook message attached. They can click and view the video from their email or log back in to Facebook and watch it from there.

Posting Video on Someone's Wall

A riskier but potentially more fulfilling way to share video is to post it on a customer's Wall. Imagine someone Liking your page and mentioning your product in passing, so in turn you post on his or her Facebook Wall the latest viral video.

There are several downsides here:

- Not everyone allows others to post on their Facebook Wall.
- It requires taking the time to go to this person's page and post it.
- The user may feel violated or used.

All that said, a well-placed video could make someone's day. Damon is really into food and, as his Facebook friends know, he talks about it a lot. He adores certain brands and, if those companies posted a cool video on his Wall, he would be both excited and flattered. But that's just him.

WATCH OUT

Before you dive into viral media, be sure to check out our later discussion on Facebook policies. Some maneuvers are actually illegal in Facebook's code of conduct. Check out Chapter 15 to get a good overview of what you can and can't do.

Integrating YouTube with Facebook

Alternatively, you can upload your movie to a video site, like YouTube (www.youtube.com) or Daily Motion (www.dailymotion.com), and post the link to the video on your Facebook business page.

Here's what you do:

1. Upload the video to your favorite video site, such as YouTube.
2. Copy the website URL from the browser.
3. Log in to Facebook and go to your business page.
4. Click the **Add Post** link on your Wall.
5. Paste the URL.

One of the biggest challenges with video is keeping a steady hand. The lighter the device, the harder it is to keep balanced while recording. Consider keeping the device on a flat surface or using a tripod.

Viral Marketing

The video-sharing website YouTube is swamped with popular videos of kittens snuggling together or people doing funny things, but your goal is much more complicated than just getting video views. You also want to inform people about your service and, ideally, get them to buy your goods. You don't want to just provide entertainment, but *edutainment*.

DEFINITION

Edutainment is informative content built into a fun concept. With the best edutainment you don't even know that you're being taught something.

Edutainment is entertaining learning. Here's what you need your edutainment video to do:

- Interest people to get and keep their attention.
- Inform them of your product or service.
- Entertain them enough for them to want to pass it along to their friends.

Let's delve deeper into these three keys to creating an edutaining video.

Interest People

The first thing your video needs to do is get people interested. The very nature of viral marketing is that your customer's friends—not your business—is the group telling him to watch it. Your one and only job is to get that first person to watch it and share it with his friends.

> **FRIENDLY ADVICE**
>
> The first people to share cool content are usually highly trusted individuals called influencers. Want to learn more about what makes influencers tick? We talk about them a lot more in Chapter 20.

The best way to get someone's attention is to make your video appealing. Any of the following elements can appeal to viewers:

- Humor
- Shock
- Romance
- Counterintuitiveness
- Boldness
- Parody
- Music

Like other aspects of your marketing efforts, the type of content really depends on your audience. A raunchy commercial won't work for a conservative political candidate, while a wholesome ad wouldn't work if you're trying to appeal to alternative youth culture.

Inform People

Your main job is to get the video into people's computers and have them pass it on, but your ultimate goal has to be informing them about your business, product, or service. Both John and Damon have seen dozens of commercials that are fun and memorable, but have absolutely nothing to do with the product—and we're sure you have, too. You don't want people to remember the commercial but forget the brand.

Here are some tips for creating good videos:

- Show your logo during the ad.

- Tell a story around your brand, product, or service.

- Use characters or situations relatable to your desired audience.

- Don't lecture.

A great example is Volkswagen's 2010 Super Bowl commercial "The Force." The 60-second clip shows a child dressed up like Darth Vader from *Star Wars*. He spends the afternoon going through the house trying to use "the force" to pull objects toward him—all while his parents look at him like he's crazy. Finally, he goes outside and begins trying to use the force on his parents' Volkswagen Passat. The dad pulls out the key and uses the remote start feature on the car, and the kid actually believes he turned on the car.

Check out the ad on YouTube at www.youtube.com/watch?v=R55e-uHQna0. As of summer 2011, it has racked up more than 40 million views. Now that's what going viral is all about.

The commercial manages to get your attention while still telling you about the new product. Here are some things the ad got right:

- It's a funny and endearing look at childhood.

- It shows one of the unique features in the Passat.

- It features the car as one of the stars of the commercial.

- It is short and memorable.

- It ends with the Volkswagen logo.

FEEDBACK

Volkswagen actually released the ad officially through YouTube—and did so shortly before the actual Super Bowl aired. The risky move created even more buzz for the commercial. Viewers who were familiar with the ad recognized it and could turn to their family and say "Watch this ad! It's hilarious!"

More importantly, marketers are learning that sites like YouTube and Facebook enable people to share content quickly. The Super Bowl may attract a billion viewers, but those viewers can't share an ad they just saw. You need Facebook and other social networks for that.

Entertain People

Finally, your video has to entertain people enough so that they want to share it with their social circles. Here are some ways to help make sure this happens:

- Use a format that's easily sharable.

- Make sure it relates to your audience.

- Keep it short.

First of all, you need to make the video easy to share. Of course, Facebook really shines when it comes to passing along media to your friends, family, and colleagues. The main thing you need to decide is if it's better to share it on your company's page, on a customer's Wall, or in a message sent out to your Facebook Group. We talk more about that a little later in the chapter.

Second, you need to make sure it's meaningful to most, if not all, of your target audience. John might find your newest ad pretty funny, but he's not going to share it if he believes that his social circle won't be able to relate to it.

Third, keep it short. When it comes to TV-style commercials, the ones with the biggest impact are a minute or less. Brief videos were initially an economical choice because TV time is so expensive, but now companies are making shorter videos because of our short attention spans.

Remember two very important things when it comes to keeping it short. First, there is such a thing as too short. However, a 10-second commercial could work as long as you were able to interest, inform, and entertain within that period of time.

Second, short is relative. If you're making a video aimed at college professors, a five-minute video may be considered too short, while for high school students a minute is probably pushing the limits of their attention span. It all goes back to remembering, considering, and respecting your audience.

FRIENDLY ADVICE

You don't need a full production studio to create an amazing viral video. In fact, some of the best efforts are simple and cheap.

Recording video can be as simple as turning on your webcam, but a professional, well-done video takes time, effort, and equipment. Depending on your goals, you may decide to outsource the video development to a small ad agency or media marketing firm.

The Least You Need to Know

- When an ad goes viral, it means that it is compelling enough that the customers share it with their social circle.
- Good viral marketing videos interest, inform, and entertain.
- Make your videos easy to share, make sure they relate to your desired audience, and keep them as short as possible.
- You can put Facebook videos on your Facebook page, your customer's Wall, or send them as email through Group pages.
- Read the Facebook terms of service before you begin posting videos.

Facebook Games

In This Chapter

- Why games matter
- How games get sales
- Viewing the best games on Facebook
- Using Facebook gaming tools
- Commissioning game creators

Facebook games, which were once an online niche, are today the lifeblood of the social networking website. Millions of people log on to the website to play any of the thousands of games available on the site.

How does this apply to your business? Games can create a deeper level of interaction with your customers. You can also use games as an entertaining way to give your customers more information about your business and your services.

This chapter takes you for a walk on the fun side of Facebook. You find out all about gaming, how advertisers are taking advantage of it, and why you should seriously consider adding interactive game media to your marketing repertoire.

Why Facebook Games Matter

Gaming has exploded on Facebook. Here are some 2011 Facebook gaming facts, courtesy of All Facebook:

- 53 percent of all Facebook users play games.
- 69 percent of Facebook gamers are women.

- 56 million users play Facebook games daily.

- 20 percent have paid cash for in-game benefits.

- 50 percent of users log in to Facebook just to play games.

Based on the last fact alone, if you aren't involved in some type of game, you're missing literally half of the audience logging in to Facebook.

> **FEEDBACK**
>
> If you really want to see how quickly Facebook gaming is ramping up, check out the market evaluations of the gaming companies.
>
> In November 2009, game conglomerate Electronic Arts acquired the Facebook game company Playfish for $400 million—considered a staggering amount at the time. Less than two years later, Playfish competitor Zynga filed for an IPO for $1 billion. In other words, gaming is serious business.

Gamification

So how do Farmville, Mafia Wars, and other strictly fun Facebook games apply to your marketing? If you can get the consumer to want to spend time in your virtual world, you can have a bigger influence on their spending.

There is actually a term for it, too: *gamification*. Championed by pioneers like Gabe Zichermann, gamification is about using the best traits of gaming to bring the best out of your company's interactions with customers.

> **DEFINITION**
>
> **Gamification** is the process of taking video-game-related play systems and applying them to nongame environments.

As a classic example, think about Pepsi holding a summer vacation contest: buy a 20-oz. Pepsi, twist off the top, and see if you won! When you think about it, this is the gamification of selling soda. You might not buy a soda to win, but if you are choosing between Coke and Pepsi, it might prompt you to choose Pepsi.

The Pepsi example isn't related to Facebook, of course—or is it? The traditional soda sweepstakes contest has actually evolved, too, and we can use it to see how the internet is making gamification even more common. About a decade ago, soda manufacturers didn't just require you to buy the soda, but they gave you a code underneath the cap that had to be plugged into a website. The website, naturally, was of the manufacturer. They got you to buy their soda and visit their website—more than likely for nothing.

Today, marketers are going well beyond codes and websites. For instance, last summer Pepsi began putting *QR codes* onto its bottles. Scan the QR code using your smartphone and the phone browser opens up a special Pepsi Facebook page. It was an excellent way to get people onto its Facebook page.

> **DEFINITION**
>
> **QR codes** are square symbols that, when viewed by a special scanner, open up a webpage or image on a device. There are dedicated QR scanners, but most computers and smartphones have free QR code software that can scan the symbol.

Reaching Your Market

Pepsi Co. and other manufacturers definitely go after the younger demographic, but adults and older people definitely drink soda, too. What if you have something more narrowly focused?

Assuming you aren't selling soda, you need to determine your market before attempting to gamify your business. If you don't know your market precisely, you can't make an effective outreach plan.

For instance, if you're going after the retired AARP audience, you might consider creating a Sudoku-style game. The number-puzzle game has really taken off among older and retired people, which means that it's an excellent way to reach that audience. Creating an overcomplicated game mechanism may frustrate older gamers who didn't grow up playing video games, and a reflex-based system may be too hard for older hands.

Using Games to Boost Your Fan Base

Hundreds of companies are using Facebook games to promote their product, message, or service. Even more impressive, a handful of them have been very successful in reaching their audience as well as getting some media attention.

Making Waves Game

The family-oriented boat dealer Discover Boating took one of the more direct takes on gamification: it literally made a game comparable to traditional video games.

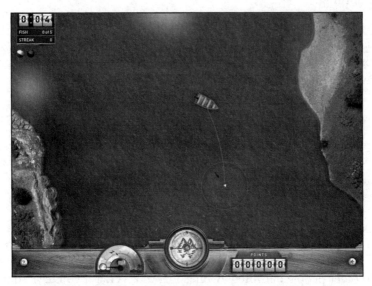

Figure 13.1: *The Discover Boating game Making Waves.*

Making Waves is a series of mini-games all related to boating (see Figure 13.1). One features players dodging buoys through a river, while another focuses on catching fish. The controls are simple enough to learn within seconds, but the art design, sound, and animation are high quality.

Making Waves works in two very important ways: First, Discover Boating took the time to create a very polished product. Second, the game itself makes boating seem fun and easy.

And when the visitor wants a break, she can just click on the info page to learn more about the Discover Boating business.

Whopper Sacrifice Game

Easily the most controversial brand-related Facebook game was also one of the most successful. In late 2008, fast-food chain Burger King launched Whopper Sacrifice.

The rules were simple:

- Delete 10 Facebook friends
- Get a free Whopper coupon

More than 200,000 people were defriended for a Whopper within a matter of weeks. Making matters even worse, when someone was defriended, Burger King would send him a notification that the friend chose a juicy whopper over his friendship.

The ruthless, sociology-driven marketing campaign got lots of coverage in the press. Some of the reports focused on the meanness of the game.

Unfortunately for Burger King, the game violated one of Facebook's terms of service. Essentially, an app cannot tell a person that she has been defriended—it is a violation of Facebook's privacy agreement.

WATCH OUT

A multi-million-dollar company, Burger King no doubt had a cadre of lawyers who let them know ahead of time that the game violated the Facebook terms of service (or at least we hope so). Burger King probably weighed the consequences and determined that it would earn enough promotion and lifetime Whopper customers to justify the risk.

Before you start your Facebook marketing campaign, make sure your plans don't violate the Facebook terms, U.S. law, or your company's ethics. Second, if you do decide to make a risky move like the Whopper Sacrifice, make sure that your company can withstand the potential fallout to your reputation, your finances, and your clientele.

Rather than change the game, Burger King opted to shut it down in early 2009. According to *The New York Times*, the chain honored the roughly 24,000 free Whopper coupons players earned during the game.

Ford Fiesta Movement

The Fiesta is one of Ford's newer car models. Compact and affordable, the car's target market is definitely the young and hip. The Ford Fiesta Movement tried to turn the car-buying experience into a big, nationwide game (see Figure 13.2).

Figure 13.2: *Ford's viral road trip for the Fiesta car.*

Ford lent 100 Fiestas to a select group of people. Each one was given a "mission"—essentially a road trip—to document with photos and video. Ford also paid for the gas. The best overall documenters would later compete to win a Ford Fiesta of their own.

FRIENDLY ADVICE

Ford was unusually bold about its intentions. Here's an excerpt from the Ford Fiesta Movement website: "For the next chapter of the Fiesta Movement—and in anticipation of Fiesta arriving in the United States—we're letting our fans take a crack at advertising. They'll use their creativity to promote the new 2011 Fiesta. And you get to be the judge."

Ford's approach is an excellent example of marketing transparency (for more on this, see Chapter 17). In short, Ford was upfront about its intentions, and its Facebook followers respected the company for it.

Set up like a real-life video game, the Ford Fiesta Movement came to America in 2011, but it previously had a successful run in Europe.

Getting Involved in Gaming

As you may imagine, getting your message out with your game can be much more complicated, risky, and expensive than just posting a video or sending an email blast.

The good news is that Facebook developers have created a blueprint for what works and what doesn't work in the social networking environment. Considering they are worth literally billions of dollars, it's worth paying attention to what's already happening and the tools they are currently using.

How Games Work on Facebook

If you want to understand Facebook gaming, look no further than turn-based strategy games, in which you make a move and then you wait for your opponent to make a move. As of summer 2011, the most popular Facebook game, the turn-based CityVille, had more than 83 million unique users a month. Other turn-based games like FarmVille and Empires & Allies had equally impressive numbers.

Figure 13.3: *Zynga has become a billion-dollar company with games like CityVille.*

The move-then-wait system works extremely well for Facebook for a couple of reasons:

• You don't have to worry about internet speed.

• You have a reason to come back every day.

Some games on Facebook have computer-controlled opponents, but the best ones have you competing against your friends. If you ask a friend to play, then you both will be visiting every day.

FEEDBACK

Having someone visit your Facebook page to play a game every day is an ideal marketing situation. Instead of sending out emails, posting on Walls, or other methods to get people's attention, visitors are coming to you unsolicited. And, unlike a News Feed, it is guaranteed that they will see whatever you're highlighting on your page.

The Financial End of Games

The biggest difference between Facebook games and other types of video games is that all Facebook games are free. You can go to Facebook right now, search for and download any game, and start playing it immediately without touching your credit card.

These guys make serious money, though, using two different methods:

• In-game purchases

• Advertising

In-game purchases are virtual, but they can be a literal gold mine for game publishers. An example is in, say, FarmVille, where you can spend the next 30 days in Facebook working on a crop, or for just a few bucks, you can instantly have the crop ready for harvest. In-game purchases are traditionally very cheap, maxing out at around $10, which just makes it that much easier for the consumer to spend a bunch of money one dime at a time.

Advertising is a great money source as well. You have a captive audience visiting your web page every single day for several minutes, if not hours. Consider FarmVille's estimated 83 million unique users. Even if they only played one minute of FarmVille a month, they'd log in 83 million minutes of ad time and, at minimum, just as many ad views.

Developing Games

Unlike other parts of Facebook, creating games requires some programming knowledge. The skill set isn't too different from what you'd need to make a game on a website or even for a mobile phone. But if you don't already have the programming knowledge, you're far better off hiring an outside developer.

WATCH OUT

Game developers, producers, and programmers dedicate their lives to understanding the craft. You don't want to end up devoting too many of your resources (time, energy, money) to the project.

Remember that your game is supposed to be supporting your main business, not the other way around.

Creating Your Own Games

If you do go at it on your own, you will definitely be leaning on the Facebook Development blog at https://developers.facebook.com/docs/ (see Figure 13.4).

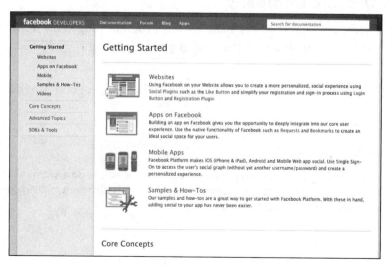

Figure 13.4: *The Facebook Development blog has lots of gaming resources.*

The Facebook Development blog is one of the most popular Facebook-related web-sites, and has lots of documentation related to ...

- Facebook websites
- Facebook apps
- Facebook Mobile apps

Games fall into the app category on the Facebook Development blog. Flip through the different tutorials on the website to gauge your comfort level. For instance, if you or your staff are uncomfortable with the basic gaming terminology, creating a game from scratch isn't the most realistic route. However, if you know games and are famil-iar with which ones work on Facebook, then the biggest hurdle is figuring out how to create the best game for your company.

If you have a clothing company, your game could test people's skill in matching the right hat, blouse, skirt, and heels. Once they put together an outfit, they can see the real-life version of the ensemble offered at your store via pictures or video. You could even offer them a discount on the outfit, like free shipping or no sales tax, if they order it right now.

In other words, make sure you understand the basics first, and then decide if creating a game is smart, or if it's even realistic for your company's brand.

Hiring an Outside Company

Facebook game creation requires some serious programming skills. From deep HTML to CSS, learning any of the programming languages could take months, if not years.

We highly recommend hiring an outside firm or, at least, a good programmer to help you get set up.

FRIENDLY ADVICE

A student at a local college or even an intern may be able to do a Facebook game for you in her sleep. Consider the local, low-cost approach before shelling out thousands of dollars to a boutique firm.

You know your needs better than anyone, so here are some recommendations for finding a good outside firm:

- Explore Facebook, find the most intriguing branded games, and find out who developed them.

- Plan your ideal outcome for the game as much as you can beforehand, even if it's just an outline.

- Chat with small companies. At this point in Facebook development, everyone is an upstart.

- Find out what games your audience likes to play. Use that to figure out which company could help you the most.

The Least You Need to Know

- More than half of all Facebook users play games, and 50 percent get on Facebook only to play games.
- Gamification is the process of applying features related to video games to non-game environments such as your business site.
- Games give your customer an excuse to come onto your Facebook page regularly.
- Facebook games are free, but they can make money by selling in-game purchases and advertising.
- Creating a Facebook game requires lots of programming knowledge, so we recommend outsourcing your gaming concept.

Facebook Apps

In This Chapter

- Getting to know apps
- Building apps
- Running an app promotion
- Going mobile
- Growing an app fan base

There are hundreds of thousands of applications (apps) on Facebook for one reason: Facebook apps make money. Users view ads, purchase virtual goods, and create other money-making opportunities for businesses. Some of the apps are free as marketing tools, and some are fee-based. If there weren't 800 million opportunities to get paid, there would be fewer apps. You can also use apps to make money indirectly, as an app could be the perfect vehicle to get customers to buy your products or use your services.

This chapter takes a look at the app business to help you decide if you should create your own app. And if you decide to get into apps, you'll find suggestions for building an audience for them.

Applications That Build Buzz

A Facebook *app* is a tool that makes it easier for customers to use your services or buy your products on Facebook.

> **DEFINITION**
>
> **App,** short for application, is any piece of software added to an electronic device outside of its standard software. The software is almost always downloaded from the internet and not added from a disk, CD, or other external medium.

Understanding How Your Business Can Benefit from Apps

So how can your business use apps? You have lots of different opportunities to get, keep, and satisfy customers using apps.

If you're a financial institution, your app could make it easier for customers to do transactions; learn about your new products; and, if they are on a smartphone, use a locator to automatically show them the nearest branch of business.

As a retailer, the app could streamline the purchasing process; show customers exclusive deals; and embed pictures, video, and sound to show the products in action.

For a public service like a fire department, a Facebook app could have interactive games that teach fire safety, videos showing proper fire prevention, and opportunities to mail reminders for, say, checking your fire alarm batteries to your Facebook friends.

Types of Apps

You can find more than 500,000 Facebook apps covering a wide variety of content, including the following:

- Web searches
- Music videos
- Family trees
- Celebrity gossip
- Discounts/sales
- TV schedules
- Birthday reminders
- Virtual gift givers
- Calendars

> **FRIENDLY ADVICE**
>
> According to Facebook, users install more than 20 million Facebook apps each day. Opportunities abound to get your app noticed!

In other words, if you name it, there is an app category for it.

Most Popular Apps

The most popular apps are as varied as the types available.

For example, the app Zoosk (www.facebook.com/zooskdating) uses Facebook to connect people on dates. Facebook is the biggest modern social connector on the planet. Zoosk simply takes advantage of it. It has more than 11 million active monthly users.

Daily Horoscope (www.facebook.com/horoscopedaily) has one of the plainest names on Facebook, but it is consistently in the top 20 used apps, with more than 12 million active monthly users.

FRIENDLY ADVICE

The most popular software on Facebook is actually games. Even the highest app, Zoosk, only has a fourth of the audience of the most popular game, CityVille.

Finally, Status Shuffle (see Figure 14.1) collects funny status updates from its users and posts them on its page. It has more than five million active monthly users.

Figure 14.1: *The funny app Status Shuffle.*

How Apps Have Gained Fans

The most popular Facebook apps seem to be all over the place. Matchmakers and humor and horoscopes have little to do with each other.

However, the top 25 apps do share the following characteristics:

- Simplicity
- Clarity
- Appropriateness

These apps are simple. Laugh if you want, but the name "Daily Horoscope" is pure genius. It says exactly what it does and the creator knew that the simple name would be enough for it to sell.

Similarly, Status Shuffle doesn't add heavy graphics or try to complicate its main goal. Instead, it simply gives users a daily laugh. It's not complicated, but it works.

Finally, each app is appropriate for its intended audience. Zoosk targets a younger crowd, so its tone, energy, and design are all geared toward it. The audience feels like Zoosk was made specifically for it, which is why it continues to support it so heavily.

Creating Your Own Apps

Interested in creating your own apps? Unlike other parts of Facebook, there isn't an app-builder per se that enables you to easily create an app from scratch. Instead, creating your own app requires programming knowledge. You need to be fluent in a number of programming languages, including Java, HTML, and Facebook API.

Making your apps in-house may save some money, but it's important to consider the time and energy commitment required to learn programming.

The pros and cons are relatively simple. If you decide to do an app in-house, you have:

- More creative control
- Potentially cheaper development cost
- Added skills for future apps

The dangers are equally strong:

- Less time working on your main business

- Potential time wasted

- Needing to hire someone to finish developing the app anyway

As we discussed in Chapter 13 on Facebook Games, we highly suggest considering an outside firm or a highly skilled programmer for help. A bit of money now could save you headaches (and potentially more money) later.

Regardless of how your app is created, it will require patience to see it thrive. You need to have realistic expectations for your apps and also be willing to tweak, revamp, or even scrap the original project.

WATCH OUT

At a recent conference, a marketing expert was asked what was the biggest mistake promoters do on the internet. "Change things too early," she said without hesitation.

The problem is that promotion takes time. If you have a new Facebook app, game, or page, it can take months for it to get any type of consistent audience, or any audience at all. Dramatically changing your approach too early means that you could be annoying your current fans and losing traction with new potential fans.

Timing really is everything when it comes to apps. An advisor can help you decide when to adjust and when to give your app more time.

Making Revenue from Applications

Like games, apps provide a plethora of different ways to make money. In fact, they offer more revenue models than any other aspect of Facebook.

Apps can bring in money via the following channels:

- Advertising

- In-app purchases

- Referrals

Advertising is a solid revenue stream as the app makes users a captive audience. You have to know your audience to determine which type of advertising they would be most responsive to.

In-app purchases could be the highlight of your app revenue. Facebook makes it relatively easy to let users buy items within your app. The currency is *Facebook Credits*, a secure method à la PayPal, that doesn't require visitors to pull out their credit cards. Instead, they can just click on the desired item and have it deducted from their Facebook Credits. It creates a virtual currency system. We discuss Facebook Credits extensively in Chapter 17.

DEFINITION

Facebook Credits is the virtual currency used for purchases on Facebook. Visitors can use their credit card to buy Facebook Credits, which, psychologically, makes them more apt to spend money because it doesn't seem like they are spending real money.

The most interesting app revenue model is referrals. If you have a good relationship, they may send you business back in return. However, on the internet, the referral usually means money changes hands:

1. Send someone to a website.

2. He or she makes a purchase.

3. You get a cut of the purchase price.

A common internet example is Amazon. The massive retailer gives referrers anywhere from 1 to around 10 percent of the purchase price.

FRIENDLY ADVICE

Is your product available only through a retailer? If the retailer is doing paid referrals, your app could get you paid twice: once from the actual purchase and again for the cut from the referral. For example, Amazon gives a referral bonus if a customer clicks on a link and purchases a product.

Mobile Apps

As we mentioned earlier, apps are usually associated with mobile devices like iPhones. Your main aim may be to get your app on Facebook, but you should also consider formatting your app so it works well on the phone. In fact, some apps are made specifically for Facebook Mobile. We talk more about Facebook Mobile in Chapter 18.

Here are some of the many ways your app could benefit from being on the phone:

- Locate the nearest store location using GPS.

- Take a photo of someone using your product and automatically post it on Facebook.

- Mention the Facebook user when she visits your store.

> **FEEDBACK**
>
> According to Facebook, more than 350 million active users access the site via phone, meaning that one out of every three Facebook users access it through his or her mobile device. You should definitely consider making your app phone-friendly.

Keep in mind that mobile goes beyond phones, too. The advent of the genre-defining iPad tablet in 2010 means that even more people will be accessing Facebook away from their home computer. Apps take a while to develop, so prep your concepts within where things will be six to nine months from now. And chances are that tablets and smartphones will become even more ubiquitous.

Creating a Successful App

Ideally your app will help promote your brand, product, or service, but you actually have to promote the app itself so it can get a decent amount of users and, ideally, media attention.

Here's what your app needs to be successful:

- Emphasize the practical value of the app. People are actually overwhelmed by the number of apps out right now. They are looking for any excuse to delete your app from their Facebook.

- Create a simple, straightforward app. Visually demanding graphics and memory-hogging sound can slow down the computer—and test a user's patience.

- Customers are willing to pay for a good app. There are apps that are making millions of dollars every day. Focus on making the app good and the money will come.

- Check to see if your app is original. With more than 500,000 apps, the chances of it already being done are pretty high.

Apps can be more versatile than a standard Facebook Group page and more profitable than the average static website. The development and risk involved with creating them are only outweighed by the opportunity for serious brand recognition and impressive revenues.

The Least You Need to Know

- Even if you outsource your app development, you still need to have a clear set of goals for the app.
- The top Facebook apps share the characteristics of simplicity, clarity, and appropriateness for their audiences.
- A large group of people access Facebook on the road, so consider mobility when you're thinking about apps.
- Apps can bring in money through advertising, in-app purchasing, and referrals.

Facebook Measurement and Sales Tools

Social media marketing is important, but the end game is to get the sale. Luckily, Facebook provides many opportunities for you to close the deal. Part 4 discusses the tools at your disposal, such as check-in services that enable customers to let you (and, more importantly, their friends!) know when they're at your business, and analytics that can show you how effective a specific Facebook marketing campaign is for your business.

Facebook Advertising

In This Chapter

- Building ads you can place on Facebook
- Creating and targeting ads
- Tracking and analyzing ads
- Pricing your ads strategically

In the world of websites and social media, Facebook ads are clearly the gold standard. With more than 800 million users providing a wide range of demographic information, you're able to deliver ads to the exact people you want to reach.

If you're looking to reach a specific target market defined by age, sex, location, and/or specific activities, you have the ability to reach them with Facebook ads. This chapter walks you through the basics of setting up Facebook ads and then delves into proven ad campaign strategies. Finally, we show you how to track your ads so you can maximize their effectiveness.

Basics of Facebook Advertising

Before we show you how to build an ad, we're going to give you some background on the types of ads you can run on Facebook, how they work, and the rules.

Facebook's pricing structure for its ads is similar to other online advertising platforms (discussed later in this chapter). Facebook sets itself apart from other ad platforms in how users can interact with the ads. Facebook ads can have interactive components that enable viewers to Like an ad, RSVP to an event on an ad, and view friends that are already fans of the page the ad is promoting.

FEEDBACK

You can access the Facebook advertising section by scrolling to the bottom of any page on Facebook and clicking the word **Advertising** or by going directly to www.facebook.com/advertising.

Types of Ads

When you begin your Facebook ads, you are given a number of options for the destination of your ad. You can link your ad to any of the following elements:

- A Facebook page
- A Facebook Event
- A Facebook Place
- An external URL (any website outside of Facebook)

Each of these ad destinations has unique features and layouts for displaying your ads.

If your goal is to drive people back to your website where you have a landing page set up with information and resources, choose the external link.

If your goal is to build up your Facebook presence and still deliver great information, the smarter choice is to send them to your Facebook page (any of the tabs you may have or just the Wall), an event, or a place. These are all Facebook pages.

You need to decide on the type of ad you want to run:

- Sponsored Stories
- Facebook ads

Sponsored Stories

Sponsored Stories are social advertisements. They display recent interactions from viewers' friends with brands on Facebook in the form of an ad (see Figure 15.1).

Imagine you're looking at the Events section of a newspaper in your local community. You see a large ad for a water park that opened recently, including a picture of the park and a list of its features. But on the right side of the ad are a few of your friends' pictures and a comment from one of them that says "I went to the park last week with Ryan and Courtney. The kids loved it. They had awesome slides and it was so close to home. —Tim."

The quote from your friend closes the deal by giving you some proof in the form of a live testimonial. Most people don't care what the ad says, but the opinion of their friend or relative—now that's believable.

The layout and content of a sponsored story changes depending on the type of story you choose. Here are your options:

- "Like" stories (see Figure 15.1): these are fairly simple, telling users that their friends have Liked a page.

- "Post" stories (see Figure 15.2): these have more content and depth still relating to users by telling them what sort of information is being shared on a page.

Figure 15.1: *Sponsored Stories can entice your viewer's friends to Like your page.*

Figure 15.2: *Multiple Sponsored Stories are even more effective.*

Advertisers use Facebook ads more than Sponsored Stories, but we believe that Sponsored Stories will continue to grow in popularity once users learn more about what they're missing. As a new Facebook advertiser, this method works best if you already have a large, established base of fans, because the stories depend upon existing fan content and activity.

Facebook Ads

Most businesses use Facebook ads as a staple to build up their fan bases quickly. These ads enable you to pick a destination tab that is either your Wall or any other tab on your Facebook page. When the user clicks an ad, they are taken to the destination.

FEEDBACK

We highly encourage businesses to set up multiple tabs on their Fan pages (covered in Chapter 7) and send ads to those pages. By doing this, you can measure the effectiveness of each tab and ad.

When you link your ad to a Facebook page, the title of your Facebook ad is the title of your Facebook destination, as shown in Figure 15.3. While this can be limiting, there is no way to change this at present.

Figure 15.3: *You don't get to choose the ad title for Fan page ads.*

Alternatively, you can change the title of an ad if you're directing people to your website, as shown in Figure 15.4.

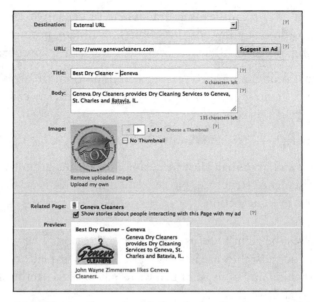

Figure 15.4: *You can choose the title for ads that direct to external websites.*

Getting Your Ads Approved

You can manage both Sponsored Stories and Facebook ads on your own without having to interact with Facebook staff. The only thing you need from the team at Facebook is for them to approve the ad. This usually happens in less than 24 hours once you submit an ad.

Facebook provides guidelines to help ensure that your ad gets approved. Facebook devotes an entire section of its site to discussing what types of ads are acceptable and what are not. Here are some of the most important guidelines:

- Landing pages must be legitimate. They cannot trap users, require that they enter information, or force pop-ups or pop-unders.

- Ads cannot imply an endorsement from Facebook. So try not to use their name, images, or references to their platform in your ads.

- The ad must relate to the page it's going to.

- The landing page cannot play audio or video automatically on load.

- Ads can't be false, misleading, fraudulent, or deceptive. In this same category, Facebook doesn't allow ads that contain, facilitate, promote, or reference the following: obscene, offensive, profane, vulgar, or inappropriate language.

- Ads can't promote tobacco products, ammunition, firearms, or weapons of any kind, gambling, get-rich scams, adult content, spy cams, and/or inflammatory religious content.

- No copyright or trademark infringements.

- Content and grammar must be clean. This means grammatically correct with proper sentence structure. No repetition in words, excessive capitalization, symbols, or punctuation.

Facebook reserves the right to refuse an ad for any reason. They are by no means trying to limit your ads; they are just trying to keep their platform clean and professional. The last thing any of us want is for this ad space to overburden the users with distasteful ads that drive them away.

To see the rest of the guidelines, go to www.facebook.com/advertising.

Building Your Targeted Ads

Now that you know a little about the parts of an ad, let's dive into the process of creating one.

You begin the process at www.facebook.com/advertising, home to Facebook's advertising section, which includes some case studies and tips.

Click the **Create an Ad** link to get started. The first page you are brought to (see Figure 15.5) guides you through the process of designing your ad. Follow these steps:

1. Choose a Destination page.

2. Select your type of ad—either Sponsored Stories or Facebook ads.

3. Choose the Destination tab. If you choose a Facebook page, by default Facebook makes the title of that page the title of your ad.

4. Insert body copy of 135 characters (one to two short sentences).

5. Upload an image and review the preview.

6. Target your audience based on various demographic data, such as location, age, gender, relationship status, and level of education (see Figure 15.6). Choose the data that best fits your target audience.

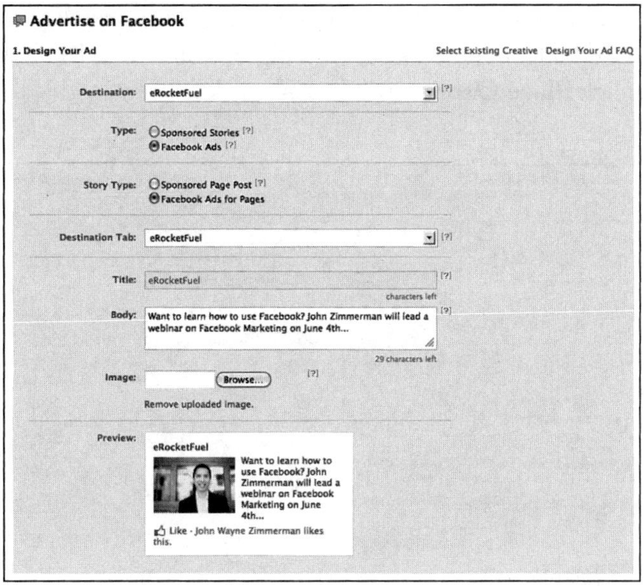

Figure 15.5: *Building a Facebook ad.*

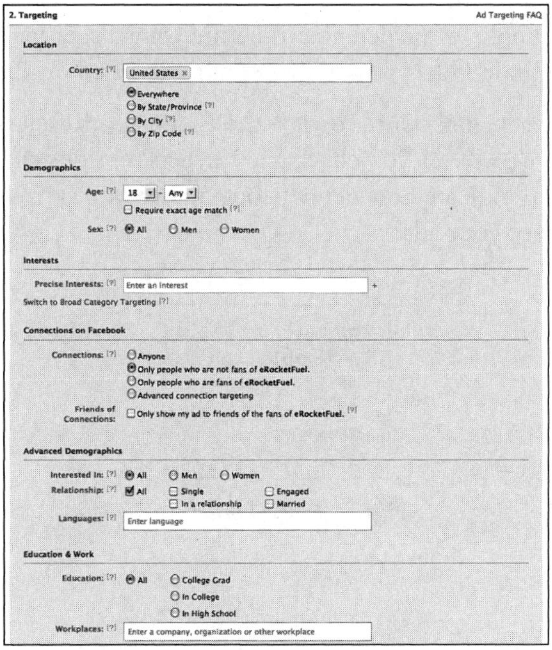

Figure 15.6: *Targeting your ad.*

7. On the Campaigns, Pricing and Scheduling page (see Figure 15.7), set your campaign budget and choose a pricing option. Click **Review Ad** to review the ad or click **Place Order** to place your order.

---

3. Campaigns, Pricing and Scheduling   Ad Campaigns and Pricing FAQ

Campaign & Budget

Campaign Name: My Ads

Budget (USD): 50.00   Per day ▾ [?]
What is the most you want to spend per day? (min 1.00 USD)

Schedule

Campaign Schedule: ☑ Run my campaign continuously starting today

Pricing

○ Pay for Impressions (CPM)
◉ Pay for Clicks (CPC)

Max Bid (USD). How much are you willing to pay per click? (min 0.01 USD) [?]
0.67   Suggested Bid: 0.52 – 0.90 USD

Note: Tax is not included in the bids, budgets and other amounts shown.
Use Simple Pricing

Place Order **Review Ad**

Figure 15.7: *The Campaigns, Pricing and Scheduling page for building an ad.*

How you target your audience is just as important as the artwork and copy. In Chapter 2 of this book, we helped you to define your target market. Now you will define the type of individuals who will see your ads based on their attributes.

As you build your ads, make sure to view the Estimated Reach box on the right-hand column (see Figure 15.8). As you check and uncheck options that define your market, this box changes to indicate how many people match your criteria on Facebook and could potentially see your ads.

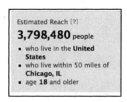

Figure 15.8: *A sample ad.*

Here are some key selections to consider when targeting your ad:

Location. Facebook enables you to choose a country, state/province, city, and a radius of that city of 10 to 50 miles. You can adjust the location to cover a narrower or wider geographic area depending on the type of product or service you are advertising. For example, if you own a small restaurant in Wilmington, North Carolina, you may want to focus the location of your ad within a 10-mile radius of Wilmington. If you're hosting a countywide festival, you might want to focus your ad within a 30- to 50-mile radius.

Demographics. Age and sex are pretty straightforward in terms of choosing people who represent your buying market. Keep in mind that if you have a product that caters to children, the children themselves may not buy the product; instead, you should target their parents, especially mothers.

FRIENDLY ADVICE

Some people don't include their age in their Profile, so select **All** to reach this audience when filling out the demographic age part of your Facebook ads.

Interests. Targeting by interests enables you to really drill down to your ideal audience. You do this by using terms people have included in their Facebook Profiles. These terms pull from users' interests, activities, education, and job titles. They even pull from pages they Like or groups to which they belong.

Because these are coming from users' Profiles, there may be multiple spellings, misspellings, and totally bizarre spellings. Facebook offers a nice feature of "Suggested Likes and Interests" that tries to find like terms.

For example, if you look up "Lady Gaga" in the Precise Interests section, you will be given Suggested Likes and Interests of "Lady gaga," "Lady Gaga Pokerface," and "Katy Perry." Notice that terms are not always spelled correctly. This is okay. The Profiles are built off of how people populate it themselves.

Facebook also includes a Broad Category Targeting tool in this section that enables you to drill down into predefined categories such as business/technology and subsets of that category such as computer programming, personal finance, real estate, science, and small business owners. It's an easy way to look at groups if you are unsure where to start, but it does limit the words you can select.

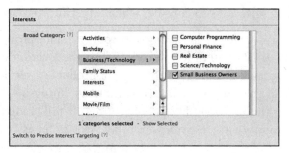

Figure 15.9: *The Broad Category Interest tool.*

Connections on Facebook. You can use this section to target people connected to pages, events, or groups that you are an administrator of. You can break this down into people who are not fans, people who are fans, and friends of your fans.

The saying goes, "It is easier to get business from an existing customer than to try and find a new customer." The same principle applies when using this Facebook tool—it harnesses the power of influence.

FRIENDLY ADVICE

We recommend using the Precise Interest Target feature in the Interests section of building a Facebook ad rather than the Broad Category tool. Precise targeting acts like a keyword Search box that enables you to be more open and precise to the words that people use in their Profiles.

In Chapter 5, you established your business's voice by first deciding on a particular celebrity or role model to copy. You can use the same strategy here to establish the persona of your audience.

You may end up creating many ad variations per campaign that you launch. We recommend using a minimum of three ads per campaign with slight changes to each ad based on the targeted audience.

Your slight changes might be these:

- Alternative images
- Adjusting the language in the ad
- Adjusting all genders to just women

Such slight changes can be very effective in generating impressions.

Cost Per Impression vs. Cost Per Click

Facebook, like most online ad platforms, enables you to purchase ads based on the following models:

- **Cost per impression (CPM)** (see Figure 15.10): You are charged an agreed-upon fee each time an ad is loaded and displayed per group of 1,000 people. This is a passive measurement with the aim of getting more visibility.

- **Cost per click (CPC)** (see Figure 15.11): You are charged on a per-click basis, meaning a user has to physically click on an ad before you are charged.

CPC is almost always the best option because it gives you a direct correlation to action. CPM can be advantageous if you're primarily interested in getting exposure for your brand. We recommend CPM for larger-budgeted campaigns of $2,000 or more a month. With a larger budget and audience reach, you will be able to learn a lot from the multiple ads you run.

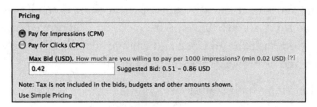

Figure 15.10: *Pay for impressions.*

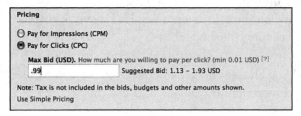

Figure 15.11: *Pay for clicks.*

Setting a Daily or Lifetime Budget

Facebook also lets you set a daily or lifetime budget, and track all of your goals. The first step to setting a budget on Facebook starts within your own organization. Online advertising budgets can range from $50 to thousands of dollars per month.

> **FRIENDLY ADVICE**
>
> You can generally get a $50 free coupon for Facebook ads by searching for it in the right places. Look for coupons in technology and business publications as well as just by searching for "facebook ad coupon" on Google.

Sponsored stories and Facebook ads are run and paid for in the same way. The way they are priced depends on what others in the marketplace are paying for similar demographics. It's all about supply and demand. As you choose your target market options, the price fluctuates based on your selection. Facebook displays a range of prices to bid on at the bottom of your ad page.

We recommend starting at the low end of the range or even choosing a number outside of the range that's slightly lower. After your ad is approved, the pricing structure changes again. So revisit the ad price and change accordingly. We've seen ads as low as 12¢ per click and as high as a few dollars per click.

You have the following budget options:

- **Daily budget:** Choosing a daily budget helps put things into perspective and is easy to monitor.

- **Lifetime budget:** A lifetime budget requires less time and effort to manage. You simply put in your budget and let Facebook run the ads as fast as they can to consume your budget.

We recommend you choose the daily budget option. You will see more benefit from your advertising investment if you run your ads this way.

Advanced Advertising Tactics

Like any type of advertising, you can test your ads' effectiveness and tweak them based on the results in order to get them to work more efficiently.

The interactive nature of some of Facebook's ads can be your greatest asset. Sometimes the smallest tweaks can make a huge impact.

Getting People to Like You

That Like button on Facebook is like crack to a Facebook marketer. The beautiful thing about the Like button is when someone clicks on it, he or she is added to a list that you can see. Short term, it's just a number that keeps climbing—but long term, it is a marketing list of people who can see your brand. The potential is the ability to market to people who are already captivated by your brand that want your products.

Facebook inserts the Like icon beneath every ad (see Figure 15.12). When users click on this link, they automatically Like your page and become a fan without even visiting it. The best part is that when they take this kind of action, you are not charged for a click.

Figure 15.12: *Notice the Like link at the bottom of the ad.*

FEEDBACK

If you choose to push your ad to an external URL, you will not be given the option of displaying the Like link on your ad.

So how do you get them to click that Like button and not the ad? There's no foolproof way to do this, but if you place content in the ad that directs people to Like by clicking on the Like link below, you will have a better chance of these kind of conversions.

An example ad might read as follows:

- Sofitel Hotels. Do you like soft beds? Click **Like** below.

- Yo Gabba Gabba Live Concerts. Is your child mad about Foofa, Brobee, and DJ Lance? Click **Like** to show your support.

- Charity: Water. What if you didn't have clean water to drink? Who would help you? Please Like the Cause. Click **Like**.

Using Images to Draw People In

Use this section to upload an image for your ad. The image should be related to your product/service, and, to make it even more compelling, it should also be related to your title/body text for the ad.

WATCH OUT

Be careful if you decide to play the sex game in ads. By placing pictures of attractive women, you probably will get more clicks and Likes. The downside is that this often brings random nontargeted traffic.

You are limited to the size of the image that you can post on Facebook, so you want to be sure to choose an image that is clearly visible when it is small. The dimensions are limited to 110×80 pixels. Additionally, the file size of the image cannot exceed 5MB.

Also, here are some ideas that might help you to select great images that scream "click on me":

- Bright colors like red, orange, and green work best to grab attention.

- Graphics with words and designs generally get more attention than pictures of people.

- Borders around pictures always increase the click rate.

- Arrows and symbols grab attention on images.

WATCH OUT

Make sure to pre-size your images in a photo program like Photoshop or a free tool like Picnik.com before uploading. If you upload an image that's not to scale, Facebook will resize it, but the focal point of the image might get lost in the automatic resize.

In the many ads we've run over the years, we have had the greatest success with ads that feature the following types of images:

- Company logos

- Dogs

- Cupcakes

Logos have worked very well with branded companies that people may recognize from multi-exposure in more than Facebook ads. The dogs and cupcakes we've run have been aimed at attracting women from their 30s to 50s.

You just never know what's going to generate a click, so we encourage you to play with and test your ads per your given business.

Writing Effective Ads

Images are particularly important because you're limited to 135 characters of text, and that text is a relatively small 11-point font.

Still, you do need to write copy for your ads. In Chapter 5, we encouraged you to divide your content among these categories:

- Informational/educational (70%)
- Selling (15%)
- Fun (15%)

We recommend using the same breakdowns when writing ad copy. Just because you're writing ads doesn't mean they have to be all marketing all the time. The most compelling marketing does not come off as selling, and so it follows that the most compelling ads shouldn't come off as ads.

Have you ever read a really compelling magazine article that you didn't notice was an ad until the very end? Maybe at the top or bottom of the page it was identified as a special advertising section. It was an ad, but disguised as content. This is how you want some of your ads to read. Not all of them, mind you, but a majority of them.

In order for you to make a connection to the people reading the ads, you need to relate to them on their level and in their language.

Measuring Success with Ads

You can access and manage your Facebook ads at any time by clicking the **Ad Manager** or **Ads** link appearing in your Applications menu, at www.facebook.com/ads/manage/.

The Facebook Ad Manager is the section of Facebook that enables you to create, edit, and delete ads and run performance reports on your ad campaigns. The ad manager might come off as being a little intimidating when you first look at it.

We're going to make this section easy for you and only focus on the parts that you as a business professional need to know to see if you are performing well, what some signs of distress are, and how to change them to get better results.

The Ad Manager

Within your Facebook Ad Manager (see Figure 15.13), you might come across a lot of terminology that you're not familiar with. Here's what all the jargon means:

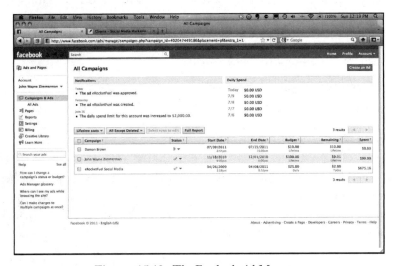

Figure 15.13: *The Facebook Ad Manager.*

- **Campaign:** A group of ads

- **Status:** Shows whether an ad is live or paused

- **Impressions:** The number of times an ad was displayed

- **Social Impressions:** Impressions that contained a viewer's friends who Liked your page, event, or app

- **Social %:** The percentage of impressions where the ad was shown with information about a viewer's friend(s) who connected to your page

- **Clicks:** The total number of clicks the ad received

- **Social Clicks:** The total number of clicks the ad received that contained a viewer's friend(s) who Liked your page, event, or app

- **CTR:** Click-through rate; the number of clicks divided by the number of times it was shown

- **Social CTR:** The number of social clicks divided by the number of social impressions

- **CPC:** Cost per click; the amount spent divided by the number of clicks

- **CPM:** Cost per thousand impressions; the amount spent divided by the number of impressions

- **Spent:** Amount spent per the given time period

- **Reach:** Number of people who saw your ads

- **Frequency:** Average number of times each person saw your ads

- **Social Reach:** Number of people who saw your ads that contained a friend who Liked your page, event, or app

- **Connections:** The number of people who Liked, RSVP'd, or installed an app 24 hours after viewing your ad

- **Unique Clicks:** Number of people who clicked on your ads

- **Unique CTR:** Number of people who clicked on your ads divided by the number who saw your ad

When you first create an ad, you will place it into a campaign. Name your campaigns by category.

Let's say you want to run a few ads intended to increase membership to your subscription website. You might call the campaign "Membership." This way you can easily manage your ads at a glance to see their impact on your campaign goal.

After you run an ad, the Facebook Ad Manager starts collecting data on it, and you can start downloading reports within 48 hours of the launch.

To review a single ad in a campaign, click the ad name and details appear below it. This enables you to compare the performance of different creative elements, review your targeting and audience size, and make valuable optimization decisions, all without leaving the page.

Three Report Options

Facebook's ad metrics can show you how your ads are reaching real people, not just how many impressions you're getting. You can get to these reports by going to www.facebook.com/ads/manage/reports.php.

You have three options on the kind of reports you can run from your report manager:

- **Advertising Performance report** (see Figures 15.14 and 15.15). This report gives you information about your ad's performance such as impressions, clicks, and conversions.

- **Responder Demographics report** (see Figures 15.16 and 15.17). This report gives you information about the users who are viewing and taking actions on your ads.

- **Conversions by Impression Time report** (see Figures 15.18 and 15.19). This report shows the number of conversions organized by the impression time of the Facebook ad a conversion is attributed to. The statistics are categorized by the length of time between a user's view or click on the ad and the conversion (i.e., 0–24 hours, 1–7 days, 8–28 days).

The report manager also enables you to download and export data that you can then customize in your own format.

WATCH OUT

If you're an advanced user, you should build your own spreadsheet or database to keep track of your ad statistics. You never know when you might need this data, and you don't want it tied up on Facebook alone.

Generating an Advertising Performance Report

Running an Advertising Performance report on a campaign enables you to see what is and isn't working.

To run a daily Advertising Performance report for a particular ad campaign, follow these steps:

1. Go to www.facebook.com/ads/manage/reports.php.

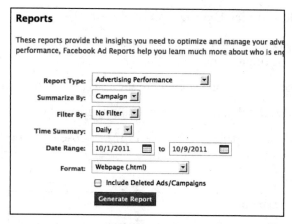

Figure 15.14: *Running a Facebook Advertising Performance report.*

2. On the Reports page (see Figure 15.14), choose the report type **Advertising Performance**.

3. Choose summary by **Campaign**.

4. Choose **Daily** for the time summary.

5. Select the date range you want to measure.

6. Choose your format. We recommend **Webpage** to make sure you are getting exactly what you need before exporting it.

7. Click **Generate Report** to see the report (see Figure 15.15).

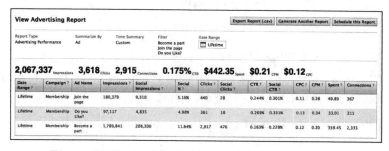

Figure 15.15: *A Facebook Advertising Performance report.*

Generating a Responder Demographics Report

By running a Responder Demographics report on a campaign, you are able to see who is actually clicking on your ads.

To run the a monthly Responder Demographics report, follow these steps:

1. Go to www.facebook.com/ads/manage/reports.php.

2. On the Reports page (see Figure 15.16), choose the report type **Responder Demographics**.

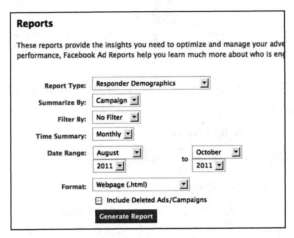

Figure 15.16: *Running a Facebook Responder Demographics report.*

3. Choose Summarize by **Campaign**.

4. Choose **Monthly** for the time summary.

5. Select the date range you want to measure.

6. Choose your format. We recommend **Webpage** to make sure you are getting exactly what you need before exporting it.

7. Click **Generate Report** to see the report (see Figure 15.17).

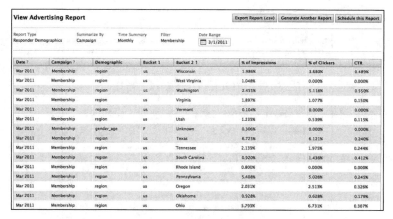

Figure 15.17: *A Facebook Responder Demographics report.*

Generating a Conversions by Impression Time Report

By running a Conversions by Impression Time report on a campaign, you are able to see how long it is taking for users to take action on your campaigns and ads.

To run a monthly Conversions by Impression Time report, follow these steps:

1. Go to www.facebook.com/ads/manage/reports.php.

2. On the Reports page (see Figure 15.18), choose the report type **Conversions by Impression Time**.

3. Choose summarize by **Campaign**.

4. Choose **Monthly** for the time summary.

5. Select the date range you want to measure.

6. Choose your format. We recommend **Webpage** to make sure you are getting exactly what you need before exporting it.

7. Click **Generate Report**.

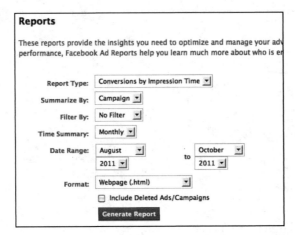

Figure 15.18: *Running a Facebook Conversions by Impression Time report.*

Interpreting Your Reports

On the report (see Figure 15.19), you can sort each column by clicking on the title of the header in any of the reports. Here are some sections that you should focus on in each report:

Date ?	Tag Name	Campaign ?	SKU	Conversions ? ↑	Post-Imp (0 to 24 hours)	Post-Imp (1 to 7 days)	Post-Imp (8 to 28 days)	Post-Click (0 to 24 hours)	Post-Click (1 to 7 days)	Post-Click (8 to 28 days)
May 2011		Membership	like_page_inline	892	2	2	0	888	0	0
Mar 2011		Membership	like_page_inline	795	3	1	2	789	0	0
Jun 2011		Membership	like_page_inline	659	0	0	0	659	0	0

Figure 15.19: *A Facebook Conversions by Impression Time report.*

Impressions. This shows you the total number of times your ad appeared on Facebook. It's likely to be the largest number on your report. In order to gauge this metric, you have to ask yourself if the number of impressions is high enough to really say anything about the ad and the campaign. If you are running multiple ads within a campaign, you will notice that although they may have all started at the same time, some ads received many more impressions than others.

Facebook doesn't guarantee any set number of clicks or impressions. They attribute a number of different factors, including competition for the audience you're targeting.

The Facebook system selects the best ad to run based on the CPC or CPM that you have set, as well as your ad's past performance. If your ad has performed well in the past, it has a better chance of showing up in the future.

If you want to increase your clicks or impressions on a given ad, you can raise your price maximum CPC or CPM.

In the Responder Demographics report, look to the age of users and their percentage of impressions. This will tell you if you need to change your target market, to zero in on the people who take action the most.

Click-through rate (see Figure 15.20). Click-through is what you're paying for when you take out ads on Facebook. When you get above a 1 percent click-through rate, you are rocking it out. Focus on the ads with the highest click-through rate to get them more exposure, which will increase your other metrics, such as the connections and unique clicks.

Date ?	Campaign ?	Ad Name	Impressions ?	Social Impressions ?	Social % ?	Clicks ?	Social Clicks ?	CTR ? ↑
Apr 2011	Recertification	CEU courses	3,794	297	7.83%	16	3	0.422%
Mar 2011	Membership	Become a part	140,545	7,080	5.04%	474	49	0.337%
Mar 2011	Membership	Do you Like?	97,117	4,835	4.98%	261	16	0.269%
Mar 2011	Membership	Join the page	180,379	9,310	5.16%	440	28	0.244%
Apr 2011	Recertification	Top of your game	19,821	1,451	7.32%	47	9	0.237%
Mar 2011	Recertification	CEU courses	171,913	13,391	7.79%	385	50	0.224%
Mar 2011	Recertification	Top of your game	46,566	4,062	8.72%	91	15	0.195%
May 2011	Membership	Become a part	749,555	78,863	10.52%	1,379	233	0.184%
Jun 2011	Membership	Become a part	899,741	122,357	13.60%	1,064	194	0.118%
Mar 2011	Recertification	Rock On	4,339	576	13.27%	5	1	0.115%
May 2011	Certification	Discover the CMA	210,082	23,597	11.23%	242	41	0.115%
Apr 2011	Recertification	Rock On	883	104	11.78%	1	0	0.113%

Figure 15.20: *Finding the CTR of your ads is key to ad performance.*

CPC or CPM. No matter which campaign you run, the reports will show both of these metrics. Compare each report to see which ad is the most effective. You can tell which one is more effective by looking at what you spent per ad, and how many viewers you got to look at the ads. Your goal is to get the most views.

Connections/Conversions. This metric tells you how many people liked your business after seeing your ad, even if they didn't click it immediately. This is how you tell how many Likes you received.

Unique clicks. It's always good to know just how many people really click on your ad.

If you view your ad's CTR, clicks and impressions will change over time. These performance graphs will help you decide when it's time to try new advertising tactics.

> **FRIENDLY ADVICE**
>
> If your numbers are decreasing over a period of time, change your ad's text and image to keep it fresh and interesting for your audience. Old images may fail to keep performing the way they did in the past.

Testing Ad Variations

You need to create multiple campaigns in order for your ads to succeed on Facebook. Thankfully, Facebook makes this task easy. From the Ad Manager, when you click **Create an Ad**, you are brought to a page called Advertise on Facebook. Click **Select Existing Creative**.

This option gives you all of the prior ads in a frame and enables you to select any of them to replicate in part or in whole (see Figure 15.21). You can view these by individual campaign or view all of your ad campaigns. To select the ad you want to work with, check the box next to it. Facebook creates a new ad for you based on the ad you chose. You can then edit the ad as you see fit.

All of the previous ad details will already be filled in the ad form fields.

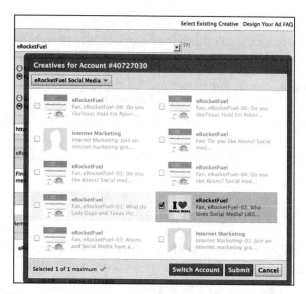

Figure 15.21: *Choose which campaign you want to replicate.*

Here are reasons you need to run multiple ads and campaigns and compare their effectiveness:

- Variability creates a higher likelihood that your ads will succeed.

- Running the same copy with different images can help you see which ad is more effective. Continue to run the higher-performing ad, and remove the other.

- Changing copy will help you to see if some words resonate better with your audience.

- Adjusting your target marketing enables you to see which demographic or interest gets more actions.

FEEDBACK

Facebook has an in-depth section on their website that teaches you all about the latest and greatest ad features. Make sure to visit this, as they add new features on a regular basis. Learn more at http://www.facebook.com/ads.

Testing ad variability is an art and science for today's marketers. They do it not only for Facebook ads but for everything they market. Play with this section and you'll discover how much impact your ads can have.

In an ad campaign John Zimmerman ran for the American Association of Medical Assistants, they spent 3 months on ads with 20 different ad variations. They were able to go from paying $1.75 per ad down to 17¢ per ad by weeding out the ads that weren't getting great social action. The result of the ads achieved over 4,000 Likes with a total cost less than $2,000. You can do this, too. It just takes practice.

The Least You Need to Know

- Traditional Facebook ads are more popular than sponsored ads, but don't let that keep you from using this underappreciated marketing tool.
- Properly targeting your ad's audience is as important as your ad's artwork and copy.
- When pricing ads, start at the low end of the suggested price range or even slightly lower.
- While CPC is almost always the way to go as it gives you a direct correlation to action, CPM can be advantageous if you're primarily concerned with getting brand exposure. We recommend CPM for larger-budgeted campaigns.
- Graphics such as logos and written words generally get more attention than pictures of people.
- Creating multiple campaigns enables you to compare the performance of your ads and refine them based on what works and what doesn't.

Your Page Analytics and Measurements

In This Chapter

- Learning how to use Facebook Insights to measure fan activity on pages, websites, and apps
- Exploring statistic tools outside of Facebook
- Tracking Facebook activity with your web stats software
- Calculating your return on investment

You have several tools at your disposal to measure page activity on Facebook. Most of these reside within the Facebook Insights dashboard. Other options include tracking via third-party software services.

Facebook Insights

Facebook Insights is a dashboard that provides reports of user demographics, Likes, and shares that occur on your Facebook page. A dashboard is a high-impact visualization of statistical data that shows the performance of a particular product so you can make more informed decisions. This dashboard is available for administrators of Facebook pages with at least 30 fans. You can use the data generated by Facebook Insights to improve your page by analyzing trends within user growth and demographics, consumption of content, and creation of content.

Discovering Facebook Insights

Facebook Insights enables you to analyze how users engage with your Facebook pages. By watching what they click on, share, and not share, you can alter your marketing plan to have greater impact. Insights provides updated reports on a daily basis and is made available within 24 hours after the full day is complete.

You can access Facebook Insights by going to www.facebook.com/insights (see Figure 16.1).

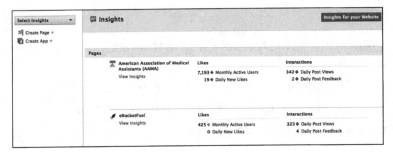

Figure 16.1: *Facebook Insights' main screen shows you all of the pages you administer.*

You can also access the Insights directly from the Facebook page by clicking **View Insights** in the top-right column (see Figure 16.2).

Figure 16.2: *The View Insights link resides on the right column on your Fan page.*

The Facebook Insights dashboard provides you with a list of all of the pages and applications you have administrative access to. The dashboard includes the following information:

- The name of the page

- The previous day's activity and whether it has increased or decreased from the day before (indicated by a green upward-pointing arrow or a red downward-pointing arrow)

- The number of active monthly users

To access more detailed information, click **View Insights** below the name of each Facebook page. Insights displays a Page Overview.

Navigating the Page Overview

The Page Overview provides a snapshot of activity on your page for the current week and month of your pages activity (see Figure 16.3). It is broken down into the following sections:

- **Users:** Features a graph with trending lines of daily, weekly, and monthly users. It also includes the number of new Likes, *lifetime Likes*, and active users for the time period you select.

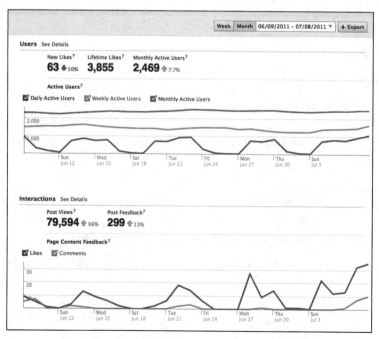

Figure 16.3: *The Facebook Insights Page Overview.*

- **Interactions:** Features a graph indicating how comments and Likes trend with each other. It also includes the number of post views and post feedback for the time period you select.

DEFINITION

A **lifetime Like** is the total number of people that have Liked your page.

Click **See Details** in each of these sections to drill down even further into the data.

When you click **See Details** in the User section, Facebook displays the following data:

- Total page Likes (number of fans)
- Daily active users
- New Likes
- Unsubscribers (Unlikes)
- Like sources (places where users can Like your page)
- Demographics (gender, age, country, city, and language)
- Page views and unique page views
- Tab views
- External referrers
- Media consumption (video, audio, and photos)

When you click **See Details** in the Interactions section, Facebook displays the following data:

- Post views
- Post feedback
- Daily story feedback (Likes, comments, unsubscribers)
- Daily page activity (mentions, discussion posts, reviews, Wall posts, video)

That's a lot of data points to look at, and all of it can be valuable. Generally, you want to look at it to derive what content encourages engagement, and then create more posts like these.

Here are some of the more valuable insights we recommend you take advantage of:

Fan Growth Per Month: Review the number of Likes (fans) you have on the first day of every month. The fan growth per month metric will show you month-over-month growth and compare it to the growth goal you established in your marketing plan (see Chapter 3). If you hit it, great—pat yourself on the back and then get back to work. If you didn't, spend some time identifying new opportunities.

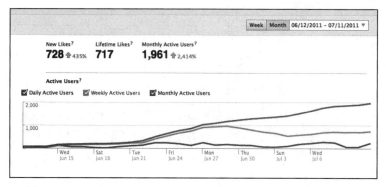

Figure 16.4: *Pay attention to the total Likes as they grow or decline.*

Likes and Comments Monthly Average: These engagement measurements (see Figure 16.4) are key to knowing whether your marketing efforts are paying off. Your posts either rock or they don't—watch these measurements as they give you the fuel to make immediate changes.

Unlikes: Monitor the number of people who unsubscribe from your page, and always try to pin down what triggered it. Two primary reasons for being Unliked are as follows:

- A topic in a post or feedback to that post that was disagreeable to the user that week. For instance, if you made a rude comment about a local politician that your fans disagreed with, they may Unlike your page.

- Failure on your part to deliver value to your clients. For instance, if you only post messages about how to buy your products and services, fans might get tired of the sales pitch and Unlike your page.

WATCH OUT

When you fail to deliver interesting content, users will get bored, which puts you at high risk of being Unliked. Prevent this from happening by staying on top of your reports and making adjustments based on the information in those reports.

Demographics: Sex, age, and location of your fans can be useful in determining if they are in fact your target market (see Figure 16.5). This report lets you know if you are in fact attracting the people you think you are. Businesses sometimes mistakenly assume that their audience on their Facebook page is the same audience that they have been marketing to offline. You can check the demographics of your audience to find out just who you're dealing with.

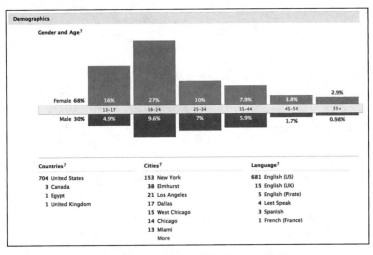

Figure 16.5: *The Facebook Insights Demographics report.*

Page Views: Page Views (see Figure 16.6) is a standard web statistic that tells you how many people came to your page, how many of those visits were by unique users (rather than the same person revisiting the page), and how many people frequent the site on a daily/weekly/monthly basis.

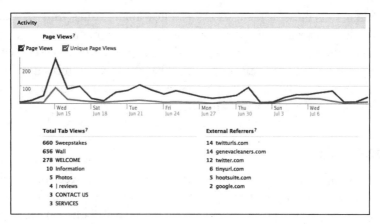

Figure 16.6: *The Facebook Insights Page Views report.*

Total Tab Views: This metric breaks down the statistics for each tab you have built on your Fan page, including custom tabs and even the default tabs like Photos, Discussions, and Wall.

External Referrers: This metric shows you where people are coming from—other websites, search engines, blogs, and so on—to get to your Fan page.

Mentions: This metric measures the number of times a fan has tagged you in a post. When someone tags you, the name of your page appears as a link. This gives your page great visibility on your fan's personal page.

FEEDBACK

When a colleague mentions your business or one of your products or services out in the real world, she is influencing her friends and acquaintances. Mentions on Facebook work the same way. When people share a link or post your page name, it puts a new message into their personal Facebook News Feed and gets their activity on your page out to a lot more people.

Tab Views: This metric is very useful for gauging the success of your custom tabs. If you have multiple tabs, this measurement tells you which tab gets the most traffic. Use this to decide if a tab needs more visibility, or should maybe be hidden or removed.

Referrers: This measurement tells you where the traffic to your page is coming from. Use this to determine where to place more marketing efforts. If a particular site brings you a ton of traffic, continue to market there; if not, reassess that site to see if there's an issue or if you should stop marketing on that site.

Impressions: This measurement shows you how many times your post has been viewed. You'll notice that it doesn't match your total number of fans due to the fact that Facebook doesn't show your posts to all fans in the News Feed. That's because the fan might have hidden your Feed or that Facebook has removed it due to inactivity. Use this metric to see what posts reach more people. Reduce or eliminate postings that reach the least number of people.

Website Insights

Facebook also offers Insights that connect to your business website by tracking when users click on a link in a post from your page to your website (see Figure 16.7). You are able to see how many posts people saw that contained a link back to your site and if they took action on the post by clicking on the link or sharing it. If someone shares a link, the report even shows a demographic breakdown per age group and gender, what language they use on Facebook, and what country they live in.

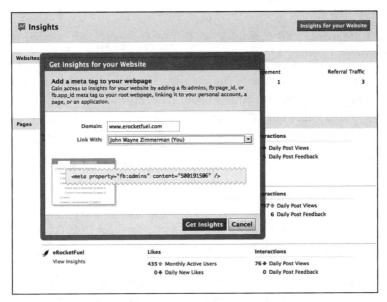

Figure 16.7: *Get Insights for your website.*

To view Insights for your website, you must first set up your domain by connecting it to your Facebook account, page, or app. Here's what you do:

1. From the Insights dashboard, click the green **Insights for your Website** button.

2. Type your domain name, link it to the account, page, or app. Linking the page to your account allows only you to see the stats. If you connect to a page or app, then all administrators can see the domain stats.

3. A *meta tag* appears at the bottom of the Insights domain setup. Copy this tag and paste it into the <head> section of your website on the homepage, and then click the blue **Get Insights** button.

4. Facebook takes a minute to verify your domain. When verified, your domain appears on the Facebook Insights dashboard on the left side of the page at the top. It will take 24 hours before you see any traffic.

It supplies you with stats on any Like buttons, Send buttons, *organic shares*, and comment boxes you have on your website.

> **DEFINITION**
>
> A **meta tag** is information inserted into the programming on your website that is used to communicate information that can tell an internet browser what to display or record.
>
> **Organic shares** are a measure of how many people shared your site link with others.

App Insights

Facebook also offers Insights for your apps should you decide to develop any (see Chapter 14). These reports track how users are interacting with your app. Some of the measurements include:

• Feedback for stream stories. These are the actions that users may take on your app that would post to their Wall. For example, a user plays a game, and a post appears on his Wall that says, "John just played Texas Hold'em Poker."

• Referral traffic to your app. This is traffic that comes from users clicking on links from the stream stories.

- A breakdown of what user actions contribute to active user count. This may include clicking links, Likes, or sharing posts.

- Demographics on users.

- The number of times permissions are prompted and granted. In order for the action to occur, a user must give their permission by clicking a link, giving permission for the app to post on their Wall.

On a support level, the app reports provide diagnostics for your app to track any errors. The errors contain messages that enable you to review your programming of the code in the app to look into what may be causing the error so you can fix it.

You can access insights for your app on the Facebook Insights dashboard or within the Facebook Developers section. The Developers section for apps can be found at https://developers.facebook.com/apps.

> **FEEDBACK**
>
> To find out more about Facebook apps, review some of the best case studies at https://developers.facebook.com/showcase/.

Your Analytics Toolbox

In addition to Facebook Insights, you have a few other ways to measure your page activity. These include weekly emails from Facebook, your own website statistics package, and third-party software packages.

Insights Emails

Each week Facebook Insights emails Facebook page administrators usage reports (see Figure 16.8). These emails are similar to the Insights main dashboard and contain the following information:

- Total monthly active users and the change in volume in the past week. By listing the number of active users, you can see how many out of the total number of users are actually engaging with your page.

- Total number of users and the change since last week.

- Activity of your fans on your page and their change in the last week.

- Number of visits and their change in the last week.

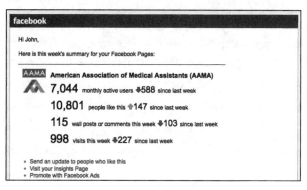

Figure 16.8: *Facebook Insight emails are sent weekly.*

 FRIENDLY ADVICE

To ensure that Facebook Insights emails don't get caught in your spam filter, add facebookmail.com as an approved domain to your address book or spam folder rules.

If you're an administrator to multiple pages, the email will report on all of your pages in a single email.

The Facebook Insights emails also include the following three links that encourage you to take various actions to improve your usage:

- **Send an update to people who Like this.** This is a reminder to regularly update your fans with new messages. The link sends you back to your page, where you can make a new post.

- **Visit your Insights page.** This brings you to your Insights main page, where you can review more in-depth statistics.

- **Promote with Facebook ads.** This brings you to the advertising section of Facebook, where you can create a new ad.

Website Analytics

Web analytics packages are software programs that enable you to track how many people visit your website, where they are coming from, what devices they are coming on, how much time they are spending on your site, and dozens of other key metrics.

Additionally, most web analytics providers have started offering more in the way of tracking Facebook and other social media sites statistics. This means you can integrate your web analytics package with your Facebook tabs.

While Facebook Insights shows some great statistical reports about fan interactions, you can go even deeper by tracking your pages with a full analytics package.

We recommend you use Google Analytics, which is a free tool offering sophisticated and comprehensive data. Here's what you do to add Google Analytics to your Fan page tabs:

1. Create a Google Analytics account by going to www.google.com/analytics, clicking **Access Analytics**, and then clicking **Sign Up**. Google asks you to supply some basic info about the website you'd like to monitor. To finish the account setup process, agree to the terms of service displayed on the screen, and click **I accept. Create account**.

2. Google gives you a tracking code to paste onto your pages. It is labeled "Web Property ID."

3. Copy this code and paste it onto every Fan page tab you want to monitor. Insert it immediately below the <Head> tag. Statistics will be available within a few hours on Google Analytics.

If you already have a Google Analytics account, all you need to do is copy the tracking code from your Google Analytics account and place that on your Facebook page tabs.

Other Facebook Analytics Providers

As you might expect, other statistics providers—both free and fee-based services—slice and dice the data in different ways. Although Facebook Insights and Google Analytics do the trick for most businesses, don't discount the other providers of similar services.

Try some of the Facebook statistics providers to see what you might be missing. In some situations, it's nice to have customized reports based upon the exact metrics you need without having to sort through a bunch of data.

Three of the four covered in the following section not only provide analytics for your own Facebook page, but the analytics of other sites, including those of competitors. Facebook Grader doesn't offer this service.

Facebook Grader

Facebook Grader is a fun Facebook analytics tool. The site enables you to grade your Facebook account and Fan page score. The tool runs a utility that scans your account or page for the number of fans you have, the power of your network of fans, the completeness of your page, and other proprietary metrics. They then give you a score out of 100. This free service can be found at http://facebook.grader.com.

WATCH OUT

We group Facebook Grader into more of a fun, bare-bones Facebook statistics package. While it may be sophisticated on the backend to pull in relevant data on which to base its ranking of your site, we don't recommend using it as your primary marketing tool. It is useful for telling you if you are way off in your marketing efforts.

All Facebook Stats

All Facebook Stats is a business analytics tool that offers a simple dashboard with a number of automated processes (see Figure 16.9). It's effective at looking at several pages at once and comparing them to each other. They offer free and paid versions and can be found at www.allfacebookstats.com.

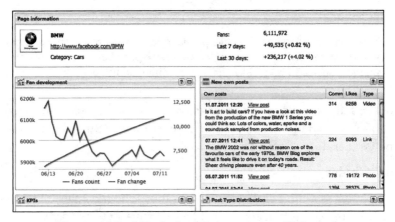

Figure 16.9: *A Facebook statistics report on All Facebook.*

Skyttle Friends

Skyttle Friends is one of the most powerful Facebook statistics tools available (see Figure 16.10). It enables you to monitor your Facebook presence, campaigns, and competitors. It integrates conversational data into simple and easy-to-review dashboards. Their reports enable you to get a deeper insight into your fans' discussions, behavior, and the activities surrounding your brand. This free service can be found at http://friends.skyttle.com.

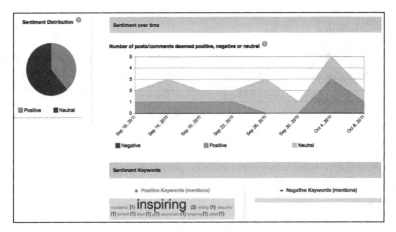

Figure 16.10: *A Facebook statistics report on Skyttle Friends.*

Social Bakers

Social Bakers is one of the largest Facebook statistics tools and covers a wide variety of Facebook statistics (see Figure 16.11). They focus on measuring and reporting on Facebook data, including Facebook in different countries, Facebook pages, Facebook applications, and Developers on the Facebook platform, as well as Facebook advertising prices. It's also effective at looking at several pages at once and comparing them to each other. They offer free and paid versions and can be found at www.socialbakers.com.

You can find a wide variety of powerful analytics tools that cover not only Facebook but other social sites as well.

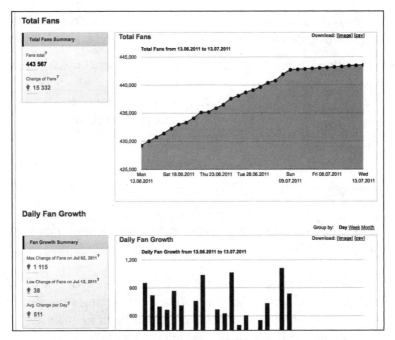

Figure 16.11: *A Facebook statistics report on Social Bakers.*

What's Missing in the Measurements?

You can access a lot of great data about your Facebook page, but some important details simply can't be found in computer-generated reports.

This section helps you answer some tough marketing questions that you won't find an answer to in any canned report.

One of the most frequently asked questions by businesses is this: *Does Facebook marketing have a return on investment (ROI)? If so, how do you measure it? And how are other companies measuring it?*

The reality of any marketing profit comes down to what was made minus what was the cost to make it. It's fairly easy to get a handle on your expenses. In Facebook marketing, your costs may be your staff's time, some consultant or agency time, and some advertising dollars.

Regarding revenue, these are the results that spurred from any actions taken on part of your Facebook marketing efforts. We like to think of revenue in terms of hard dollars and soft dollars:

- **Hard dollars:** Revenue you can track via specific links that you use within your campaigns, special codes, and exclusive Facebook-only offers.

- **Soft dollars:** The sales generated based on personal touch points that occur through engagement and interaction. Much like a sales person who is talking one-to-one to a client, how your Facebook page connects with users is hard to quantify, but we all know it's important. It takes the right finesse, delivery, and cunning to close any deal with a customer.

> **FEEDBACK**
>
> Link-tracking websites like www.Bit.ly, www.Owl.ly, and many others enable you to type in a long URL, and this site will shorten the link and provide you with click-through statistics.

The ROI in hard dollar value is very real, and can and does happen all the time for companies that take the time to address Facebook marketing strategically. The ROI in soft dollar value is very real, too; however, it is difficult to quantify. You just have to trust that it's there, working for you behind the scenes.

The following sections help you answer some other key questions.

How well is the competition doing?

If you're BMW, how do you fare against Audi or Mercedes?

Most people would simply do a lookup on the number of fans and compare that total number. What you really need to do is go beyond fans and dive into which company has the most active fans from the right demographic who talk about your brand with a positive sentiment.

All Facebook, Skyttle Friends, and Social Bakers can help you dig further than any built-in tool that Facebook currently offers on its site to manage statistics.

Who are my top fans?

Victoria's Secret has over 14,000,000 fans. But who are their biggest fans? Wouldn't it be nice to know if you could pull out the top 5 percent who spend the most money per visit, are most active on their Facebook page, and are most likely to scream from their pink polka-dot panties that they love the brand?

You can determine these kinds of fan attributes by keeping track of all of your posts and recording/comparing the data to your current customer base. There is no automatic way to do this just yet, but you can do it manually.

What are my fans worth?

You might end up spending a sizeable investment your first year in Facebook marketing to get it right. With all that effort, can you put a price per fan?

You can calculate a price per fan by looking at the impressions generated in the News Feed and applying average ad pricing to the number of Facebook fans you have.

FEEDBACK

According to a new study by Virtue, the average Facebook fan is worth $3.60 in earned media.

How many of our fans have become customers?

You can always find out the answer to this question the hard way and implement tracking codes to every link you post on Facebook, and go into Google Analytics and review where links came from and if they followed the path all the way on your website from Facebook to Checkout on your site. But why not just ask them?

Use any of the following methods to verify if your customer is a Facebook fan:

- Simply ask them on your checkout form.

- Use the Question tool and ask people on your Wall.

- Pull a list of your customers and compare it to your fans.

How effective are my ad campaigns?

You may be running Google ads that push people to Facebook, or Facebook ads that push people to your site or Fan page. You can track all of these and, even more, the organic growth.

Nearly every question in this section can be answered if you integrate your Facebook marketing efforts with the rest of the organization. The key is to tie your data points and bring in different product owners and to track it all.

The Facebook Graph API also enables you to track many of these with just a little programming and creative flair for analytics.

What It All Comes Down To

When considering the costs and benefits of social media marketing, always keep in mind that the expectation within social media is that you're there for your customers, and your hope is that they will like your brand, product, or service so much that they will influence others to give you business. So when it comes to the marketing measurement of ROI and actions, keep in mind that calls to action aren't as important as influencing actions. Your job as a Facebook marketer is to influence fans' intent to purchase a product. When done effectively, this can be a huge win for you.

The Least You Need to Know

- You can use Facebook Insights to analyze content consumption. By watching what users click on, share, and don't share, you can alter your marketing plan to have greater impact.

- Insights can also help you to track how people are using your Facebook apps, how many people are using them, and what amount of reach and viral capacity they are achieving.

- You can install scripts from Google and Facebook Insights that allow you to tie your website and Facebook together so you can see how many people go to your site from your Facebook page activity.

- In some situations, it's nice to have customized reports based upon the exact metrics you need without all the sorting with an exported table report by using third-party software sites.

- When it comes to the marketing measurement of ROI and actions, calls to action aren't as important as influencing actions.

Selling on Facebook

In This Chapter

- Keeping your relationship open and honest
- Knowing when to ask for the sell
- Considering storefront design
- Making money with Facebook Credits
- Using Open Graph

Facebook is open and free, but it takes a lot more than slapping up a storefront and a digital shopping cart to get the recognition, sales, and success that your business deserves.

In this chapter, you find out how to get customers to actually purchase your product, snap up your service, or stay connected to your brand. It all comes down to engaging with your fans from beginning to end. And once you've finally landed that elusive customer, we give you some ideas for how to keep them loyal.

Sell Products on Facebook

When it comes to selling your products or services on Facebook, the most important thing to remember is that it isn't an online marketplace like Amazon.com, which is built from the ground up for commerce. People go onto Amazon to buy, but they go onto Facebook to connect. After they connect with you, you can discuss a sale. Up to this point in the book, we've focused on making the connection. Now it's time to start thinking about the actual sale.

So how do you get the sale on Facebook? It comes down to the following major decisions:

- When to be direct and when to be discreet
- Knowing when to ask for the sale
- Deciding between Facebook sales tools and third-party software

Let's take a look at these choices.

Marketing Transparency

Facebook has brought interesting sales terms into the forefront, one of them being marketing transparency. You may recall from Chapter 2 that marketing transparency involves a business giving a customer an incentive to buy without actually engaging in the hard sell. Because Facebook is a social medium, it gives us a greater opportunity to connect with our audiences and give them something more than just a quick sale. Ideally, marketing transparency builds a relationship with the client that leads to multiple sales down the line.

Here's how marketing transparency works:

- You create a free or low-cost service to the public.
- You help the client discover why he or she needs the service.
- You mention a discount for the service or a product in exchange for a longer-term commitment.

For example, let's say you're a restaurant owner planning to launch a happy hour. It's easy to advertise "Half-off drinks!" just like every other liquor-licensed establishment in your city, but you want to build a relationship with your new customers.

Instead of focusing on happy hour, you can give the customers more bang for their buck. As an example, if you want the jazz crowd, you could have a music trio come in occasionally for happy hour. Your advertisements, whether on Facebook, in the newspaper, or on a flyer, would advertise the free entertainment along with the happy hour prices.

FRIENDLY ADVICE

Make sure your promotion is targeted toward the audience you want. For instance, if you want to get your high-end restaurant known among the upper crust of society, you probably don't want to do an open mic night, but you could feature a local painter's "tasteful" work on your Wall and have a party celebrating the exhibit on opening night.

After a few weeks of happy hours, you can monetize your audience and advertise your restaurant in many ways, including the following:

- **Create a lunch discount:** Attend three happy hours and you get a free side order at lunch. Advertise the special discount through your Facebook page.

- **Raise the happy hour prices:** Ultra-low happy hour prices can be a loss leader for more profitable happy hour prices later. By then, the audience will be coming for the free music and won't mind paying a little extra. If people question the pricing, you can say you'd like to give extra to the great band.

One successful example is Leland Tea Company, a small, but busy café in San Francisco. A couple years ago the owner began hosting Iron Cupcake, a play on the popular television show Iron Chef, where bakers are given a mystery ingredient and they have to make the best cupcake featuring it. The ingredients vary from chocolate to curry, bringing heavy discussions on the Leland Tea Company Facebook page and curious new customers to the little tea house for the free monthly event.

They even created a serious buzz and brought in people who later became regular customers.

The Direct Approach

Alternatively, it's sometimes best not to beat around the bush. Yes, we're big fans of marketing transparency, but the direct marketing approach can truly highlight the best parts of your business, including:

- Your business's personality

- Your business's service or product

- Your customer timeline

For example, if you own a garage, your customer is going to think of you only when he needs his car repaired. When you first meet, the customer is likely going to be in the midst of a crisis and isn't going to be interested in building a relationship.

As a result, your Facebook marketing needs to be more direct than, say, a growing church or a budding department store. For instance, the garage could give priority service to customers who Like its Facebook page. Or customers who check in to the business on Facebook (we discuss check-ins in Chapter 18) get a free car inspection.

When to Ask for the Sale

The best time to ask for a sale is when the client is engaged. To get a client engaged takes time. In other words, getting to the right sale time takes patience.

Remember that people come to Facebook to communicate. It could take several discussions and maybe even some freebies on your part to get a customer, not to mention a loyal customer.

Facebook Marketplace

Facebook may not have launched with commerce at the forefront, but the creators have added tools to make sales easier. One of those tools is the Facebook Marketplace (see Figure 17.1).

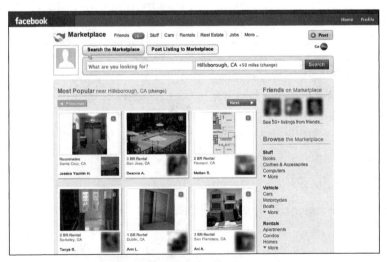

Figure 17.1: *The Facebook Marketplace.*

The Facebook Marketplace is more similar to eBay or Craigslist than a commercial site like Amazon.com. Items are organized by type, such as car or home.

When someone logs in to Facebook and visits the Marketplace, items are shown based on the user's location. Facebook also prioritizes items that are posted by friends and friends of friends.

Any Facebook user can also upload his or her own items to sell. You include the following information:

- Item/service being listed
- Price
- Location
- Category
- Photo(s)
- Description

Facebook also uses a website called oodle (see Figure 17.2) for more professional sales. For a price, oodle will help you do the following things:

- Determine your ROI
- Advertise quickly on Facebook as well as other social networks
- Communicate more easily with Facebook customers

Figure 17.2: *Facebook's advertising service oodle.*

The twist? Depending on your sales category, oodle will cost you oodles of money. As of summer 2011, car-related sales on Facebook oodle ran up to $499 per month.

oodle is worth looking into if you'd rather spend money than time. Otherwise, you may be better off putting your resources toward your Facebook marketing strategy.

Store Integration

Facebook may not be the most elegant marketplace, but smart retailers have built their storefront from or even within the social network.

With the right programming, you can put your website inside your Facebook page. Think of it as a minisite. A minisite is a small, pop-up website dedicated to a specific event or product release. It's separate from the company's main website, but connected to it through links.

For example, when Warner Bros. launches the latest Batman movie, it doesn't convert its main WB site into a Batman-only site, nor does it embed the Batman movie website deep inside the main site. Instead, Warner Bros. creates a minisite, like BatmanReturnsAgain.com.

Here are some of the advantages of creating a minisite:

- Stronger brand identity for the product
- Clearer web results for people looking for the product
- Less clutter on the main company website

You can look at your Facebook presence as a minisite: a way to get customers more intimately involved with your company and services, but not a replacement for your other media.

Anatomy of a Facebook Store

You can set up your Facebook minisite in numerous ways. For example, the couture-line Nine West has a highly interactive Facebook page at www.facebook.com/ninewest.

Unlike most other Facebook pages, the main page of the site is occupied by a full, clean image. You can immediately tell that it's a sale and, with the Eiffel Tower design, it's likely on a high-end, exclusive product. (You might be able to make that out in the cursive in the screenshot.)

The Wall postings that usually appear on the front page are still there, but they've been pushed to the left-hand column along with these options:

- Wall
- Info
- Sweepstakes
- Shop Fanshop
- Spring/Summer 2011 Tote Illustration Contest!
- Tote Poll

The user just needs to click on the left-hand column to go to the appropriate page.

> **FEEDBACK**
>
> When designing your Facebook store, determine what your audience needs the most. A website targeted at teens might want a prominent Wall to make sure its heavily social clientele can chat. An adult-focused website like Nine West knows its audience is more interested in shopping than chatting on its site, so it puts the Facebook Wall at low priority and emphasizes the exclusive discounts and quality products.

What's also great about this page is that it encourages viral promotion. The Sophie Theallet sale featured here says the following: "Like us to view & show the exclusive, limited edition collection."

In other words, if you Like Nine West on Facebook, you'll get exclusive access to merchandise. It's a nice example of marketing transparency—Nine West isn't doing a hard sell, as it already knows you're interested. Instead, it's giving you something— exclusive access to the goods—for free, all for the click of the Like button.

In turn, Nine West gets two things:

- **Free advertising:** When you Like something on Facebook, it's announced on your News Feed for all your friends to see.

- **Higher chance of sale:** Nine West is essentially making potential customers work a little to access some exclusive goods. Once users take the time to Like Nine West, they are accessing what seems like a privileged area, and they may be more likely to buy something.

Outsourcing the Creation of Your Store

Tweaking the Facebook template to create a custom site like that of Nine West requires a bit of programming. We're all for do-it-yourself work, but don't be afraid to grab a programmer or a tech-savvy associate to help you along.

If you decide to outsource your minisite, try to work with reputable companies already established within the Facebook world. Here are some that we recommend (with a shameless plug for one of the author's own companies):

- **8ᵗʰBridge, Inc.** www.8thbridge.com

- **Fluid** www.fluid.com

- **MoonToast** www.moontoast.com

- **eRocketFuel** www.erockfuel.com

Alternatives That Work

Minisites are cool, but you don't have to hire a programmer or reinvent the Facebook template to make a sale.

If you have already developed your main website and are happy with its sales process, you can simply use Facebook to link to your primary company site.

Alternatively, if you'd like to drive more traffic to your Facebook page, you can link from your company website to Facebook.

The best way to connect your Facebook page to your company website and vice versa is by using the Facebook *API*, or application programming interface.

> **DEFINITION**
>
> **API** stands for *application programming interface.* It is code that creates faster communication between different software programs. Well-written APIs enable you to access a software's power without having to get your hands too dirty with all the technical stuff.

The API is a collection of programming shorthands that make it easier for Facebook to communicate with other websites, including your own. The Facebook API has been available for years, but in 2010 the programming suite got a major overhaul and was renamed Open Graph.

Open Graph

On April 21, 2010, Facebook CEO Mark Zuckerberg hopped on stage at his F8 Developers Conference and let everyone know that his website wanted to organize the internet. Why can't you link your Facebook stats, for instance, to your Yelp or Tumblr statistics? He argued that the only true way to understand web patterns was to have one unifying set of data. The new Facebook API *Open Graph* would do just that.

> **DEFINITION**
>
> **Open Graph** is a Facebook application that enables users to interact with the rest of the internet.

Using Open Graph, you can use Facebook logins and data without having to ask your customer to input any info themselves or having to create and store your own database. It's like using Facebook's power without having to set foot in Facebook. Open Graph streamlines the connection between your site and Facebook virtually automatically. Drop Open Graph into your website and it does the following takes:

- It recognizes if your visitor is a Facebook user.

- If your visitor is a Facebook user, it automatically checks to see if he or she is logged in.

- If logged in, the user can comment on your blog under his or her Facebook name.

> **FEEDBACK**
>
> Open Graph isn't limited to websites. In fact, many mobile apps use Open Graph to get user information. By using Open Graph, their customers can dive right into the app. It also makes it easy for the app to post news onto users' Walls—ideally with their permission!

To install Open Graph, you need to have a little HTML know-how. Facebook provides a few lines of code that you plug in to your website HTML. After you plug in the code, the Like button displays on your website and, when a user clicks on it, "So-and-so likes your company" displays in his Facebook Wall.

Open Graph provides a great way to get more exposure for your company, product, or service. Let's say you are a record company releasing a new single from an artist. You can install Like buttons on the artist's personal website, the company's corporate website, the websites of the company's other artists, and so on. Each Like appears on the user's Wall, which will make the user's friends curious about the artist.

> **WATCH OUT**
>
> When you click on the **Like** button on any website where the Facebook Like is installed, Facebook posts your Like to all of your friends on your Wall and, depending on the Like programming the page used, it could post your picture and your name on their Facebook feed. If you're concerned about this privacy issue, be careful what you Like.

Facebook Credits

Facebook Credits are the website's secure way of doing transactions (see Figure 17.3). They are most often used for virtual goods.

Figure 17.3: *Learning about Facebook Credits.*

Let's say your friend is having a birthday and you'd like to put a teddy bear on her Facebook Wall. Certain apps will enable you to put virtual gifts on her Wall for anywhere from $1 to several dollars.

These transactions were initially done by credit card, but Facebook Credits now lets customers make secure purchases with one click.

Your business can still use credit cards, too, but there are a few solid reasons to use Facebook Credits instead:

- Your customer likely already has his or her credit card info or PayPal account stored within Facebook Credits.

- Facebook Credit gift cards can be purchased at physical stores like Wal-Mart and Target.

- Customers are more likely to spend more "abstract" Facebook Credits than traditional credit card currency.

Like Open Graph, setting up Facebook Credits requires knowledge of HTML/ JavaScript.

This is one of those cases where it's worth the money to outsource these details instead of handing them yourself. However, if you're feeling adventurous or would like to steer your hired programmer in the right direction, you can visit https:// developers.facebook.com/credits/ for several pages of code you can copy and paste into your Facebook website.

The Least You Need to Know

- People come to Facebook to interact, so to generate a sale you first need to engage with your users.
- It might be useful to think of your Facebook page as a minisite of your main company website.
- A custom Facebook page requires some programming that you can outsource.
- Open Graph enables Facebook users to Like your product or website outside of Facebook.
- Facebook Credits are a safe, secure way for customers to spend money on your business within the Facebook website.

Local Business and Facebook Places

In This Chapter

- Setting up your local business on Facebook
- Using Facebook Places
- Creating Facebook Deals
- Linking the local and online community
- Getting ideas for deals

Facebook can help you get customers from nearly any internet-connected place in the world, but lately it's helping businesses connect locally, too. Companies are embracing Facebook's local features because they realize that the Facebook marketing platform is powerful enough to attract the person down the street as easily as it can the remote customer.

This chapter tells you all about the location-based Facebook Places, the discount service Facebook Deals, and other ways companies are using Facebook's international platform to attract local customers.

The Small Business and Facebook

A funny thing happened as we all got connected on the internet—we suddenly wanted to embrace our local community. Seemingly overnight, Facebook became ground zero for local businesses promoting their services and products.

In 2011, Facebook started rolling out tools to allow *hyper-local content*.

In embracing local communities, Facebook made it easier to make these sorts of connections:

- Customers to find local businesses
- Businesses to find local customers
- Businesses to offer special deals to local customers
- Customers to *check in* at their favorite locations

> **DEFINITION**
>
> **Hyper-local content** is information that's only pertinent to people within a certain community. The term usually applies to physical communities, not virtual ones.
>
> **Check in** is when a customer uses a mobile device to let friends know that he or she is visiting a particular establishment. Checking in is done via a social network, such as Facebook, or a check-in app, like FourSquare. The check-in is shared with the customer's friends, which creates advertising opportunities for the business.

A Step Ahead

Books like the one you're now reading wouldn't have been as relevant even a few years ago. Not only was Facebook in its infancy, but businesses were still trying to get their bearing online. Granted, having a website was standard, but other technologies and concepts were barely around, if at all:

- QR codes
- The iPhone
- The iPad
- YouTube

> **FEEDBACK**
>
> Many businesses saw a serious loss in profit during the economic downturn that begin in 2007. Smart business owners knew that they had to make use of new technology to survive. Without the recession, many companies wouldn't be pushing to be as innovative as they currently are.

Local Community

The Facebook change is also a reaction to the wildly popular check-in services, in which people can tell their friends, families, and even their favorite companies where they are located. Arrived at your favorite bar? Check in on your phone and your friends know that they can meet you there. Check in at the airport? Your family now knows that you've touched down in your hometown.

These are two major check-in services:

- FourSquare
- GoWalla

However, numerous other apps and websites have embraced the check-in concept, including Facebook, Google, and Yelp.

FEEDBACK

Checking in to a place requires a smartphone with apps or a solid internet browser, like the Apple iPhone or a Google Android phone. Your audience will not be able to check in if the majority of them have an outdated phone.

For now, you can probably imagine the impact check-in services have had on local businesses. The quiet diner at the corner now has busy rushes when a particularly popular person on FourSquare checks in there. The local barbershop can cut its advertising budget because Yelp check-ins keep it popular on the rating's website.

Point of Sale

Finally, mainstream America has gotten very excited—some argue too excited—over mass-market coupons. Over the past couple of years, online companies began offering deals for half-off various services. For instance, you may get an email for a local restaurant offering a $40 meal for $20.

The two leaders in the mass-market coupon field are Groupon and Living Social.

FRIENDLY ADVICE

Coupons are a huge business—and the big tech companies know it, too. In fact, in late 2010, Google reportedly offered Groupon $6 billion to be purchased outright. It was even more shocking that Groupon refused, reportedly because it thought the number was too low.

And a bunch of other companies are getting in on the action, too, including these:

- Yelp
- Google
- Open Table
- TravelZoo
- Facebook

The deep-discount deals are mailed to millions of subscribers, so a local business could get a huge uptick in traffic from just one daily coupon. Facebook recognized the power in encouraging local commerce.

Facebook Places

Facebook Places is essentially the social network's spin on check-in services (see Figure 18.1). This is the step-by-step process:

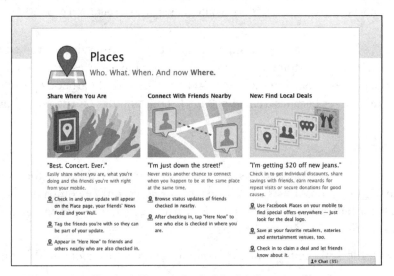

Figure 18.1: *Facebook Places let's you "check in" at your favorite venue.*

1. Go to a venue.

2. Open Facebook or the Facebook Places app on your smartphone (see Figure 18.2).

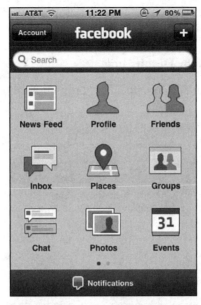

Figure 18.2: *The Facebook smartphone app.*

3. If you are using the Facebook website, click **Places**.

4. Facebook lists all the nearby registered venues (see Figure 18.3).

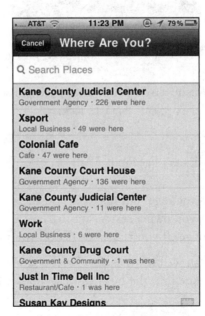

Figure 18.3: *Facebook Places lists all the venues close to you.*

5. Select the venue where you are by clicking it.

6. Tag any friends who are there with you.

7. Click the **Confirm Details** link.

8. Facebook announces your location on your Wall and on the venue's Wall (see Figure 18.4).

Figure 18.4: *Checking in to a venue using the Facebook app.*

Facebook Places distinguishes itself from other check-in services by offering the following features that other check-in services lack:

- Tagging friends
- Posting on a business's Facebook Wall

Check-in services are all the rage, but not every business can take advantage of a Facebook Places page. If you own a restaurant, bar, or retail store, you should have an active Facebook Places page. If you run a law office, you might not benefit from one.

For instance, if you run an ice cream parlor, Facebook Places would allow customers to check in when they come into the business. Facebook check-ins allow users to provide commentary, such as, "Raymond's Ice Cream has the best chocolate sundaes ever! It always makes my day." The check-in appears on the user's Facebook Wall, as the user's Facebook status, and on your Facebook Places page.

Businesses can encourage their customers to use Facebook Places and check in to their store. In return, the business can enter customers into contests for prizes. A local dry cleaner may say "Check in to Facebook Places while we are checking you out. Win free dry cleaning." A beauty salon might market Places by saying, "Check in on Facebook at Hilda's Hair and Be Part of the Gossip." A vet clinic might offer $5 off your bill for checking in. A theater could offer free posters, or even points that lead up to free admissions, free soda, popcorn, or Junior Mints.

Create a Facebook Place

As a business owner, to take full advantage of Facebook Places, you must first set up your Places page online. Signing up for a Facebook Places page is a multi-step process, but it's relatively straightforward.

WATCH OUT

Facebook has a verification process for setting up Facebook Places, but savvy techies may be able to fool the website into thinking that they're the owners of your business. Go ahead and set up your Facebook Places page right now, even if it remains dormant. Lock down your Facebook Places page while you can.

Here's what you do:

1. Go to your business location and open Facebook on your smartphone.

2. Click **Places**.

3. Click **Add**.

4. A window appears, prompting you to type in the venue description including name, address, phone number, and other information that may be of interest to customers.

5. Confirm the details and click the **Confirm** icon.

6. Type in your business name in the Search bar.

7. Open the Facebook Places page.

8. Click **Is this your business?**

9. Facebook will verify that you are the business owner by phone, usually within a few days.

After Facebook confirms your identity, you can edit the page with your address, telephone, and other data.

Integrating Your Places Page with Your Facebook Page

Facebook automatically integrates your Facebook Places page into your current business page as long as you use the same address for both. A Facebook employee verifies the address, so the process isn't instantaneous.

> **FRIENDLY ADVICE**
>
> While you're waiting for your business pages to sync up, why don't you make sure your main page is accurate? The wrong address, phone number, or email could result in lost business.

Facebook Deals

Why go through all the trouble to do Facebook Places? It enables you to make Facebook Deals. These coupons can help bring customers your way—and bring them back, too.

Facebook Deals come in these four varieties:

- **Individual Deals:** These are essentially standard-issue coupons. You post the deal on your Facebook Places page, and if a user is interested in the deal, he buys it and uses it when he's ready.

- **Loyalty Deals:** These deals reward customers based on the number of times they check in to your Facebook Places page. For example, you might offer customers a 5 percent discount on the fifth time they check in.

- **Friend Deals:** These give customers a gift for getting their friends to check in, too. For example, you might offer a customer a free meal if she checks in with five friends.

- **Charity Deals:** These deals provide incentives for the customer to spend money by offering to donate money to various charities. For example, you might donate $5 to the local school district for every $50 a customer spends.

FRIENDLY ADVICE

For Loyalty Deals, Facebook limits the minimum number if check-ins to two and the maximum to 20. In other words, you can't make a deal that rewards someone for checking in once, or a deal that requires more than 20 check-ins.

Setting Up a Deal

When you're ready to make a deal, head to your Facebook Places page; if it's already integrated with your Facebook business page, you can access it directly from that page. Then follow these steps on the screen that appears (see Figure 18.5):

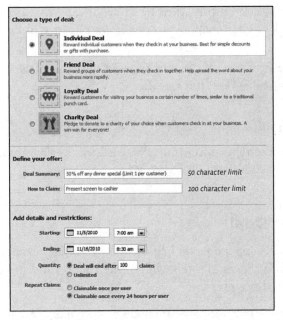

Figure 18.5: *Setting up your Facebook Deals.*

1. Click **Deal**. Facebook prompts you to make the following selections:

2. Click the button next to the type of deal (Individual, Friend, Loyalty, or Charity) you want to run.

3. Define your offer by adding a brief summary of the deal (limited to 50 characters) in the **Deal Summary** window and instructions for claiming the deal (limited to 100 characters) in the **How to Claim** window. Try to be as specific as possible when describing how to claim the deal. For instance, you could have a customer claim a deal by showing his phone to you, by printing out the coupon beforehand, or by saying a particular code. Being clear here will save you from a lot of potential trouble later.

4. Choose a Starting and Ending date and time using the drop-down menus.

5. Limit the number of claims by clicking the button next to **Deal will end after [number] claims** and adding a number; if you don't want to limit the number of claims, click the button next to **Unlimited**. Make the number too small and you don't know if you could have had a more successful campaign. Make it too large or, for that matter, unlimited, and you could run yourself out of business.

6. Limit the number of claims per user to once or once every 24 hours by clicking the relevant button. Murphy's Law dictates that people will try to take advantage of your coupons, so this is your chance to limit their activity.

After you choose from one of the four types of deals, you have to describe it in 50 words or less. Try to be brief but specific.

FRIENDLY ADVICE

Certain coupon elements can be modified later, but it's always best to have your plan set before announcing the coupon.

Promoting Your Deal

The real work of issuing a coupon begins when you start promoting it. Ideally, you want a few key influencers to catch wind of the coupon and share it with all their similarly influential friends.

Facebook does make promoting your coupon easier than, say, advertising in a newspaper. Here are some options:

• Share it via a Facebook status update

• Create a viral video for the sale

- Contact influential bloggers
- Advertise the sale at your place of business

Great Ideas for Deals

The sky's the limit when it comes to deals through Facebook. Here are some suggestions for executable deals.

- Give a discount for customers who Like your Facebook page.
- Give customers who mention your product on their News Feed exclusive access to a special Facebook sale.
- Use a funny, obscure holiday relevant to your product as a theme for your sale. For instance, on International Talk Like a Pirate Day, you can have a nautical-themed sale.
- Give a special item to the person who checks in the most during the course of a week.

The Least You Need to Know

- Facebook is more supportive than ever of local businesses.
- Facebook Places and Facebook Deals provide check-in services and mass coupons that can be used as free advertising and to attract new customers.
- If you establish your business on Facebook Places, then people can check in to your venue and use your online deals.
- There are four types of Facebook Deals: Individual, Loyalty, Friend, and Charity.
- You can set the parameters for Facebook Deals, from the length of time to the number of coupons for sale.

Mastering Facebook

Facebook is an ever-evolving website, so you'll need to continually update your basic skills to keep your Facebook presence fresh and current. Part 5 provides the advanced ideas and concepts you need to stay on top of your game, including how to integrate Facebook fully into your bigger marketing plan, ways to make a tighter social media team, what to look for when outsourcing your media strategy, and ways to cultivate the best public image possible.

Your Social Media Team

In This Chapter

- Building a well-rounded team
- Establishing the rules of the road
- Defining team roles and responsibilities
- Handling emergencies and responding to negative comments

By now you have probably come to realize that while the principles of social media are fairly simple, the execution takes manpower to monitor multiple sites, engage with users in creative ways, and respond to their posts. You can't do it all by yourself. You need a team to make your social media soar to new heights.

In this chapter, we go over what your team is responsible for: strategy, execution, and owning social media within your company. Let's go over the details on how to make the best team for your business.

Putting Together a Social Media Team

One of the very first things you need to consider is who will own social media within your organization. By *own*, we mean who will ultimately be responsible for when things go right—and when things don't go as planned. In many organizations, the website is owned by the marketing department and supported by the information technology (IT) department. If you have a small business, these "departments" probably have only one person in them. If you only have one person on staff, you need to train that person to have a wide knowledge of the organization's products/services and clear communication skills, and give them the authority to speak on behalf of your business.

If you have a larger company, we recommend creating a cross-disciplinary team to manage your social media. Why? Social media affects many departments and a larger trained team can best utilize the management of it.

> **FRIENDLY ADVICE**
>
> What if you run a small organization that doesn't have a marketing department? If you're in an organization with fewer than 10 people, you still need to separate out the functions needed for the smaller team. As you grow, it will be easier to separate the duties.
>
> In today's social media environment, you have no idea how quickly your business might explode.

Why You Need a Team

Thanks to Facebook and other social media platforms, customers now expect open, ongoing communication between the business and the customer. This isn't going to change anytime soon. So that means not only do you have to get used to this new level of customer engagement, you also have to plan for it and embrace it.

If you only have one person in the office who manages your social marketing, it's not scalable and can't grow at all. In fact, it may stunt the growth. You need a team to help. And that team needs to be peopled with the right employees and empowered to make decisions and communicate freely.

Your team's internal objective should entail the following:

- Working across departments within your company to make sure any Facebook posts that require others' input gets the right answer.

- The employee who is managing your Facebook account's main goal is to ensure customer satisfaction.

You need to make sure that everyone on the team is on board with your Facebook communications strategy, plan, and implementation. How do you do that? The best way to get—and keep—everyone on board is by having weekly meetings so that departments can share the following types of information:

- What is working?

- What are the challenges people are facing?

- What can be done to improve the current system?

The Stakeholders

The stakeholders of the social media team should include a member of the executive team as a sponsor, and leaders from each of the departments involved.

In your organization, this might look like a member from the following departments:

- Marketing

- Public Relations

- Customer Service

- Sales

- Product Development

- Information Technology

FRIENDLY ADVICE

If you aren't the CEO, it's a good idea to get upper management to support your social media strategy. While they may not be involved in the day-to-day activity, they need to know why it's important and how it can affect the bottom line.

It's not often that you see information technology departments on a team for social media, but we recommend doing so for a number of reasons.

First, there are often bottlenecks within an organization to get staff access to social networking websites, tools to manage the social sites, and sites used to support your social campaigns.

Second, you might need to install software to build and manage your social media presence.

And finally, if you plan on video hosting or bringing in large amounts of traffic to your site, the information technology team needs to be aware of the potential growth and have plans to support this traffic.

Having IT staff on board enables them to let you know what's technologically feasible and what isn't. Additionally, if IT staff know what you are hoping to get out of your social media, they will be in a better position to help you achieve those goals.

> **WATCH OUT**
>
> Are you familiar with Super Bowl ads? Yes, the multi-million-dollar commercials that air during the biggest football game of the year in the United States. Many times for the past decade there have been commercials aired that pointed the viewers to a website.
>
> In some cases, there was so much traffic that the website that was supposed to be a lead generation tool crashed. Oops. That's too bad because the strategy was effective in getting people to the site, but couldn't deliver the site itself. This is why it's so important to have multiple departments and skill sets represented on your team.

Choosing the Right People

What skill sets should people on the social media team have?

Although it would be great if they were all social media and Facebook ninjas, it's unlikely that this will be the case. Communication skills are the obvious answer. You are going to be picking leaders from each department, so here is a set of qualities we recommend:

- **Well-versed in all company products/services.** You want people in a company who have been there for a while and understand the culture and know what it is the company sells.

- **Positive attitude.** A positive attitude goes a long way in keeping customers happy.

- **Keen listener.** Great listening skills are necessary to be able to discern and then deliver what customers really want.

- **Problem solver.** Every social media team player is going to have to tackle difficult issues. It's the nature of customer interaction.

- **High integrity.** Because these people are going to be working on the front line with customers, they must be very trustworthy.

- **Tactful.** We all say things that come out wrong at one time or another. When employees have tact, it just comes out friendlier, and they are able to appease even the most troubled.

Establishing Team Roles

After you've identified your teammates, it's time to give them jobs. All of the jobs break down into three categories, as follows:

- **Engagers:** These are the "front end" employees who communicate with customers on an ongoing basis. They post information on Facebook and other social media websites. They start conversations and build relationships, ultimately being the connection to building friends and fans and closing deals.

- **Idea generators:** These "back end" folks write the posts and come up with the contests. They also listen to the chatter that's going on around the internet. If people are making positive or negative comments about your company or its brands, products, or services, they route them to the engagers to deal with on the company site.

- **Strategizers:** These are the folks who oversee the workflow of the team, analyze what is going on, and identify areas for improvement. Your IT team may also fit into this team so they can support you.

Dividing and Conquering

So how many people do you need on the front end to really conquer social media? You need at least 25 people.

We're kidding. Most businesses use one to five people. The more people you can place on your team, the better and more efficient it will become.

WATCH OUT

As you begin to dive into your new social campaigns, make sure you have one person online at a time per account. You don't want to step on each other's toes as you answer people. This is why scheduling is so important in your planning.

As you begin to work as a team in the social space, building a schedule of the times to listen, engage, analyze, and hold group meetings will become very important.

As mentioned in Chapter 10, most people engage on Facebook before work (7 A.M.), right after work (5 P.M.), and late at night (11 P.M.). That's when the engagers should plan to engage with them. Also, make sure to schedule activity on Saturdays. During nonbusiness hours, you can divide the task of replying to posts among employees.

We've moved into an era in which everything is fast and furious and people need answers right away. That's part of the social media landscape and what you are getting yourself into as you embrace social media. The downside is that you need to be covered around the clock. The upside is that you are now connected to your customers around the clock.

It won't take you long to figure out what scheduling system works best for your company. Starting out with a 24/7/365 social media monitoring system off the cuff might not be right for your business.

WATCH OUT

Make sure all of your employees sign social media management agreements. An agreement might entail that the Facebook page she manages is on behalf of the company, and not under control of the employee herself. Additionally, it should stipulate that when she leaves the company, she must give control back to the company. One drawback about Facebook is that any administrator of an account on Facebook can remove the other administrators and take control of the account. Protect yourself by training employees on this seriousness, and have them sign these legal documents.

Setting Up Workflow

So how should the multiple people on your team work together and in what order? They will still maintain their current company positions but they should work with their managers to identify time each week to work on their social media tasks. The most important parts to social media workflow are accuracy and delivery.

Your engagers will have most of the daily work, which might look like this:

1. Post

2. Listen

3. Respond (Draft, Approval)

4. Repeat

The engagers also have a second duty, which is to listen for conversations on a daily basis. This means that they monitor the company Facebook page at many points throughout the day and respond to requests as needed.

The idea generators have less of a daily schedule and more of a weekly process that looks like this:

1. Write (Draft, Approval)

2. Create artwork (Draft, Approval)

3. Build out documentation for engagers

The strategizers may meet on a weekly or monthly basis. Their role dictates that they get reports from the engagers on a monthly basis to see what is and isn't working on your Facebook campaigns. They then review, evaluate, and make any changes to your marketing approach.

Writing a Social Media Policy

A social media policy outlines corporate guidelines and principles for communicating on Facebook and other social websites. Its purpose is to protect the company and the employees.

It goes beyond confidentiality agreements. Is it restrictive? It can be. But it can also mitigate risk in a very open internet today where people talk about not only their personal lives, but their opinions of work.

Here are some tips when writing your own social media policy.

- List what is acceptable.

- List what is not acceptable, including postings that disclose any confidential or proprietary company or partner company information.

- Require that people read it and sign it in front of another employee. This is a serious contract and you need to share with them how serious your company is about its purpose.

- Mention that the policy applies to all social networking sites current and future: Facebook, Twitter, LinkedIn, YouTube, Google+, blogs, vlogs, wikis, and so on.

- Require that all employees use a disclaimer when making comments on behalf of the business. The disclaimer should read "… views expressed here are mine alone and do not reflect the views of my company …."

- Indicate that the company reserves the right to request that specific topics are avoided, withdrawn, and/or removed.

These are not the end all, be all, of a social media policy but it will get you started. We recommend getting an attorney to finalize your policy to ensure it is binding.

FEEDBACK

Here is a great resource for sample social media policies: http://socialmediagovernance.com/policies.php

In Case of Emergency

So what happens when there are negative posts on your Facebook page? Negative posts might take any of the following forms:

- A complaint about a product or service

- A threat to your business or an employee

- A business disaster in the making

What should you do as a social media manager?

First off, don't panic. You're in a public forum and people will be people. Some are positive, and some are negative. In some rare instances, they can actually offer constructive criticism all by themselves. If not, it's your job to make a negative comment more constructive. You can do this by asking probing questions.

Here are some guidelines when you first get a negative comment:

- Read it and all surrounding comments for the context.

- If it's a high-level complaint, let management know. If it's low, deal with this yourself.

- If the comment is derogatory and has inappropriate language in it, remove it.

- If it is just a little critical, let it stand for a while. Your fans might just do a great deed and calm the Wall with some defending rebuttal.

WATCH OUT

In case there is ever an extreme issue like threats, make sure to seek legal assistance. They can contact the social media sites to have something removed that you don't have access to.

Make sure you put guidelines for handling negative comments into your social media procedures and train your team on how to handle them. The worst thing to do is to just delete all negative posts, or to start an argument.

When you delete a comment, you have to remember that all of your fans had the opportunity to see that negative post, and if it was something they agreed with and you didn't address it, you will have lost their trust. Similarly, if you get into an argument with your fans, it reflects very poorly on your company.

The Least You Need to Know

- Good social media takes manpower to monitor multiple sites, engage, and respond.
- It's essential that you build a team even if you are a small organization.
- Don't go overboard and start a 24/7/365 social media monitoring system off the cuff—that may not be right for your business.
- It is your job to transform negative comments into constructive exchanges.

Should You Hire a Facebook Consultant?

In This Chapter

- Recognizing the right time to hire out
- Hiring the agency
- Using consultants to find influencers
- Looking at a success story

There are many reasons why you might want to explore hiring a consultant/agency that's well versed in social media marketing. They can help you plan if you're new to social media. They can help bring you to the next level of your social campaigns. And they can even help you achieve the highest success rate with some incredible social and viral approaches that you may not have considered before.

No matter what your reason might be for hiring a consultant or agency, when you choose to hire out, it's not a matter of simply handing over all responsibilities and walking away from it; you have to remain involved in order to maximize your effectiveness and influence in the social world.

Can hiring a consultant or agency be effective? Absolutely. Is it a sure thing? No, but nothing in life is. Do you need to hire a consultant or agency? This chapter answers that question, serving as your guide to knowing when it's time to take your social campaigns to the next level.

When you are beginning anything new, it often helps to have a mentor, someone who can give you that little extra encouragement. That is the one big advantage to having a consultant/agency to work with. They are familiar with the finer details of social media marketing that you need in order to get the most out of it.

If you were to take up a new sport such as bungee jumping, would you simply read a book, buy the equipment, and find a bridge? It's possible that all would work out just fine and you would have a blast doing it. Alternatively, you could end up in the emergency room or dead.

We're not saying that social media is an extreme sport, but you have to be careful before you jump in, or you might end up worse off than before you started.

What Is a Facebook Marketing Expert?

Many people use the terms *social media marketing expert* or *Facebook marketing consultant* on their resumés and CVs. It's not only individual consultants who do this but also businesses that are hoping to cash in on the social media buzz.

I'm sure there are many ways to define a Facebook marketing expert. Here is how we define one:

- Has built Facebook pages and groups

- Can explain the benefits of teasing an audience before showing them the real content on a Facebook page

- Knows how to identify a customer's persona and use it when communicating with fans and potential fans

- Has run extensive Facebook advertising campaigns for multiple clients and not only has generated thousands of Likes, but also has achieved a positive financial return on investment

- Has multiple references who can testify to the quality of their work

Just because someone calls herself a social media expert doesn't mean that she is one. Social media is not a stand-alone skill set. It also requires a thorough understanding of traditional and internet marketing.

Qualifying a Consultant

So how do you pick the very best consultant to work with you on your social media projects? Treat the process like you would if you were evaluating a new business partner. Here are some things to take into consideration:

- Look at their previous clients.
- Ask them about their biggest success.
- Check them out via references.
- Review the sites they have worked on.

All you need to do is visit the social media sites that the consultant has worked on. The great thing about social media is that all the artwork and content are present for everyone to see, so you can see how the site is set up, how the Facebook posts are written, and how the engagement is working.

> **FRIENDLY ADVICE**
>
> If you have ever hired a company to build you a website, you probably asked them for some links to sites they have built. You got the links, took a look at the sites, and formed an opinion. You either liked the sites or you didn't. Use the same tactic when evaluating social media consultants.

Here is a list of some topics you should ask social media professionals to supply you with in a reply back to your request for a proposal:

- Years in business
- Number of employees working on social media projects
- Number of total social media clients
- Range of costs from former clients
- References from former clients
- Greatest social success
- Greatest opportunity missed

When Is It the Right Time?

The right time for you to engage with a social media consultant/agency greatly depends on your immediate needs, goals, budget, and timeline.

There are many variables to consider. Following are some questions to ask yourself to get you thinking in the right direction.

- Does my team currently have the skill set to set up, design, and communicate effectively in our target social networks?

- Has my team been able to achieve goals we set forth since launching our social media sites?

- Does my team have ample time to devote to social media management, marketing, and maintenance?

- Does my team understand return on investment and have the ability to deliver analytics that make business sense?

- Do I understand everything I need to know in order to make the best decisions to move my organization forward using social media?

> **FRIENDLY ADVICE**
>
> If you have a social media goal that requires more people power and strategic thought, bring in a social media professional to help you. You will maximize your own team's time by doing so.

If you answered "no" to one or more of these questions, you would probably benefit from hiring outside help.

Budgeting Considerations

The price range of working with a social media consultant/agency varies greatly: an independent consultant may charge in the low thousands, an agency like our author John Zimmerman's charges an average of $20,000, and there are others who charge above $100,000.

The prices of social media consulting fluctuate per the needs of a project, but these are a general indicator of the market.

A Few Words About Using Interns

We see companies hire interns all the time to fill the social media role. They think that because interns are young, they must be savvy with social media.

That mentality is not well thought out. It's like saying that kids talk all the time on mobile phones so let's put them in charge of telecommunication companies. It's a mismatch to assume this.

Interns and entry-level staff have their roles, and it can be part of a social media team. They can help by listening or responding to common questions. They can also pull data and create artwork. They will need a lot of direction and guidance to make sure it meets the business objectives and adheres to your brand.

> **WATCH OUT**
>
> We've heard of many cases in which inexperienced and careless staff have put major dents in a company's reputation, either accidentally or by "going rogue" on their employer's social media channels and offended either the public, current customers, or clients. Treat your social media marketing as you would any other aspect of your business, and make sure that you put qualified individuals in charge of it.

Training Your Team

In addition to working with companies on a one-on-one basis, social media consultants and agencies often offer training on using social media such as Facebook. Companies around the world are registering their employees for online boot camps, sending them to conferences, and even bringing trainers onsite to educate the entire staff.

You have a lot of options to get more training for your team. The training options outlined in the following sections all have their advantages and disadvantages. Like any type of education, the most effective method depends on your learning style. And of course, it also depends on your available time and budget. Ultimately, they all offer great training opportunities.

Online Training

Brief tutorials to full-length social media training courses are available online. These can take the form of webinars, teleseminars, virtual conferences, podcasts, telecasts, teleclasses, and online university classes.

These are the quickest ways to learn more about social media in a very short amount of time. They are relatively inexpensive, costing anywhere from $99 and up.

Depending on the size of the class, it may not be the best option if you have a lot of questions that you want to get answered. For a brief overview, they are short, concise, and get your team information quickly.

In-Person Training

This option ranges from consultants who come to your location and train your staff, to attending a conference and participating in a social media session, to a small, customized, focused workshop.

Timing-wise, these occur on a monthly to quarterly basis with prices generally ranging closer to $499 and up.

The size of the classes can vary. Conferences may have more than 100 people in a session while workshops can have fewer than 25 attendees. If you attend one of these training sessions, bring along your social media plan and try to get feedback on it.

These kinds of events can be very advantageous and far more cost-effective than bringing on a consultant/agency for a contract.

Books, Articles, White Papers, and Websites

Social media marketing is not rocket science. You can find all you need to know on your own. It might take some time and commitment to master the details, but it's doable.

Facebook and other social media platforms offer countless resources in the Help sections on their sites, and success stories you can draw on appear across the internet on social media magazine sites, blogs, and even the social networks themselves. We recommend a few of them in Appendix B of this book.

> **FRIENDLY ADVICE**
>
> Many social media professionals offer special discounts to attend their events if you register early, are a fan, and subscribe to their newsletter.

Diving into a New Social Platform

Social networks are constantly evolving, and you need the latest information to be able to participate in them effectively. By hiring a social media consultant to help you, you will save time by not having to constantly search for what has changed. Facebook is continually updating its site in order to stay competitive with other social networking websites.

Companies sometimes start using Facebook without any real reason except that it's the biggest social network and everyone else is on it. In some situations, there might be a valid reason to seek out niche sites that are populated with a smaller but concentrated dose of your target audience. A social media consultant will be able to tell you whether Facebook is in fact the place you need to be to market your business online effectively.

Here are some areas where a consultant can help you with Facebook:

- Identifying your audience demographics and seeing how many Facebook users exist in your target market

- Finding the top influencers who have Facebook accounts

- Creating an optimized Facebook account that is visible to everyone

- Developing a process to export your Facebook fans and compare them to your list of current or prospective customers

- Giving you qualitative and quantitative proof that Facebook will work for your business

FEEDBACK

There will always be new social media platforms coming out; it's smart to do your due diligence to find out if you should be playing ball on the new field. A social media professional will be able to give you the scoop on the new site so you don't have to conduct the research yourself.

Exploring the History of Projects

If you're considering working with a social media professional, ask for some links of Facebook pages or other social networking pages that they have built, and visit those pages.

Each social network enables you to see historical conversations. They are a great way to see how companies talk and how fans/followers respond.

On Facebook, click **older posts**. On YouTube, click **view all comments**. On Twitter, just keep scrolling to the bottom of the page.

FEEDBACK

Do your homework and dig into a Fan page's history to see how successful the page has performed. Scroll to the bottom of the page and keep clicking **older posts**. If you do this during daytime hours, you will likely be able to see posts back for years. This option isn't always available at night, when Facebook is backing up its site.

The Art of Real Referrals

So here's the deal when it comes to getting references from consultants/agencies. The typical process looks like this:

1. You request a few references.

2. The consultant/agency gives you a list of them.

3. You call the references and they give you glowing reviews.

The problem with this approach is that the consultant/agency's approved client list has been prepped. I'm not saying they are running a scam, but when anyone has been prepped, the messages can come out a little canned.

Have you ever watched the TV show *Law and Order*? On the show, lawyers coach the client on what he will be asked and what he should say. The outcome is that it looks polished. People generally are not that polished in life, and when they are not it's usually when they are giving you the raw, unvarnished truth. This is probably one of the greatest things about social media. It brings out our real personas.

Here are some tips for getting authentic feedback about a consultant or agency:

- Don't just request references. Ask for names of companies that your social media professional has worked with and seek out employees with that company and talk to them via social media.

- Go a step further and cold call them. Take them by surprise and ask them for five minutes of their time. Explain to them that you are in the same situation they were and need some help in making an important decision.

- Google the company and their list of references for keyword phrases like "success," "fail," and "contest." Make sure to search the social network search engines, including the Facebook search tool.

We don't recommend calling companies out of the blue from a client list on a social media professional's website. They might have worked with the company in a capacity that has nothing to do with the type of help you're seeking.

Marketing with More Influential People

One of the greatest advantages to hiring a social media professional is that they may already know a lot of the social media industry's biggest *influencers*. That means a shorter lead-time to get some real buzz going on for your business.

DEFINITION

An **influencer** is someone whose voice and actions many people in a community respect and react to.

Beyond this, they know how to identify the main influencers in your industry. This is essential to do whether you hire a social media professional or not.

The job of the social media professional is to identify who your audience is in terms of wants, needs, and demographics and find an influencer(s) who can get your word out faster to a larger audience.

That will, in turn, create buzz, traffic to your social sites, and conversations. The job of the social media professional is also to ensure that you're prepared for high responses by setting up workflow with your team.

The Power of Influencers

Getting an influencer on board with your social media program can be the fuel you need to launch your Facebook marketing to a higher level. A social media marketing or public relations consultant can help.

One of the most important advantages of hiring a social media consultant is their experience in researching and finding influencers. It takes a lot of skill to be able to sift through the internet to find the right conversations for your industry and identify who has the largest reach and potential influence. Then, it will take some convincing to get them on board with your business to write about, endorse, or even acknowledge you.

What if you are a budding rock star and your consultant is able to get Lady Gaga to mention you on Facebook, MySpace, YouTube, and Twitter? Hello, instant *American Idol* traffic!

Let's take that down a notch to a local level. Let's say you have an ice cream shop called Grahams in Geneva, Illinois. Well, it's going to be hard to get Lady Gaga to mention how she loved the double chocolate fudge, but you could certainly benefit from local influencers.

A consultant is going to be able to identify these influencers on a national or local level. At least, that should be your requirement before hiring them. And the direction you give them will be to find local people that the local people know and trust. That might be the local Chicago news station television anchor, or maybe the business with the largest number of Facebook fans in town.

There are several categories when it comes to types of influencers.

- **Super-connectors:** Generally these are rock stars and celebrities.

- **Social elite:** These are the most active personalities online who blog, tweet, and post a video weekly.

- **Loyal customers and advocates:** These are the people who have been customers for years and love your brand. They tell everyone about it.

All of these influencers have potentially large audiences who follow them and engage with them on a regular basis. You will use their reach to get your message to more people.

FRIENDLY ADVICE

Does one particular person come to mind when you think about the heroes of your industry? Create a list of potential social media influencer candidates. They may be the only fuel you need for marketing on Facebook.

How to Find and Win Influencers

Even though you may hire a consultant to help you with this daunting task, it helps to know how they do it so you can help. Now that you are sold on this concept, you need to find as many influencers as possible and get them on board. How is that done? And what is the process?

Here are some tips to get you going:

- Search for keyword phrases that define your audience.

- Identify the list of influencers.

- Follow them and begin having conversations with them. Offer them value, not only casual conversation. Ask how you can help them.

- Bait them with stories that share what you have to offer to their audience. Be transparent. Don't sell them.

- Create conversation triggers to keep the contact active.

Repeat this process over and over again. You want to develop a system so the process is easy, but you also need to make every conversation authentic. If you come across as fake, you're not going to succeed.

A Success Story

You should start thinking about what you expect from your social media consultant. Will they just bring you more fans, or will they reach further and tap into more revenue for the business? You should expect and communicate exactly what you want. Both are possible.

The American Association of Medical Assistants (AAMA) embarked on social media in fall 2010. Like many businesses, they were at first reluctant to get involved with social media, but they also knew they needed to get up-to-date to stay ahead of their competitors. They were contemplating starting a Facebook page, a Twitter account, a LinkedIn group, and several others, but they weren't sure how to move forward.

They conducted some research to find a social media consultant who was known and trusted in the fields of health care and associations.

After many interviews, they found a match. It was our author, John Zimmerman. John and the AAMA embarked on social media and marketing planning and finally decided to focus on launching a Facebook page.

By working with a social media consultant, as of October 2011, the AAMA gained more than 13,000 active Facebook fans. These fans not only created a space for conversations, but the overall membership for AAMA increased by several thousand members.

The Least You Need to Know

- Working with a social media consultant can take your Facebook campaign to new levels.
- Consulting starts at a few thousand dollars and may even exceed $100,000.
- When deciding on a social media consultant or agency, take the time to find people who can speak honestly and openly about having worked with the company in the past.
- A social media consultant can be instrumental in getting the right influencers on board with your social media program.

Is Your Business Likeable?

In This Chapter

- The secret to being liked
- Establishing control
- Why love matters
- The power of patience and persistence
- Creating consumer trust

The core of Facebook marketing comes down to really one question: Do they like me? It sounds childish, and it probably recalls days of pimples and sweaty hands. But this is what Facebook is all about: connecting with past friends and new colleagues and becoming visible to your community.

In this chapter, we delve into what makes businesses popular, or likeable, and talk a little about what makes them unlikeable. Being likeable is key to an established presence on Facebook.

What Makes a Likeable Business?

The question that a consumer will ask regarding your business on Facebook is this: Will this company care more about making a profit than my well-being?

Translation: Do they even care about me enough to talk to me and respond to me?

Great products and services help influence people to like a business, but it's the people behind the business that really make the business likeable. Not a logo, or a cool product—although these are important, too.

Many businesses lead the market and are quite popular, yet customers don't really like them. Why is that? For one thing, there may not be enough competent competitors in the market that offer the same products and services.

Think about the financial sector. Do people really like banks and insurance companies? I've never met anyone who truly likes these kind of companies. People generally utilize such companies as a necessity. They may go to them because that's what their parents did and what everyone else seems to do.

Depending on the type of business you work for, you may be in one of these situations. Ultimately, you want to step ahead of this curve and do the things that make people really enjoy doing business with you.

> **WATCH OUT**
>
> Social media marketing has opened the gates to a more social world online. Consumers are able to reach businesses and have conversations with them 24/7 now in a form where everyone can see the conversation.
>
> If people representing the company are unpleasant or even mean-spirited, everyone sees this and it hurts the likeability of the brand.

When we think about the businesses we like the most, we think about people within the businesses that are completely selfless, who give help at a moment's notice, and who go above and beyond their normal duty.

It's the attendant at the ice cream parlor who gives me an extra large scoop of mint chocolate chip, the waiter who brings my little girl a balloon, or the bartender that knows what I like to drink and hands me my favorite beer as I sit down.

You can do the same nice gestures on Facebook, such as these:

- You can congratulate fans for any successes.

- You can supply fans with a short answer to their questions as well as a link to a page on your website, blog, or video that talks more in-depth about the topic they asked about.

- You can feature a fan of the month based on the amount of interaction on your Facebook page.

- If a fan has posted a question, and you don't know the answer, you can ask all of your fans the same question to see if they know.

- You can encourage your fans to network with each other by asking them to all introduce themselves.

By developing relationships with your fans, you will get to know them and that will make the difference in loyal fans versus just another metric. And you'll have a picture of that fan to help you remember who they are and what they look like.

Giving

At the heart of the social web is a giving community. It's people talking to people about the things in their lives that matter. For many, communities might be a local church, a group of close friends, or a charity. Businesses embrace these things as well. Their employees can take part in charity runs for AIDS patients, breast cancer survivors, and children with disabilities.

People are giving back to their social communities in time and money to make the community thrive as a whole, not because of outward appearance, but because it is the right thing to do.

When giving is authentic, people know—and that is an incredible Like factor.

FEEDBACK

Three quarters of small business said they donate a percentage of their profits to charity each year, with 5 percent of firms donating more than 10 percent of their profits.

You can share these kinds of charitable activities with your communities on Facebook. They will help to put a face to your business. People will then really get to know you. And that is when they can really start to like you.

FRIENDLY ADVICE

Facebook has a section called Causes that allows nonprofits and charities to receive donations from Facebook users. As an individual, you can make a donation to a Cause, and share the cause with your network of friends. Participating in Causes can have a positive influence on your Facebook friends and fans.

You can learn more about Causes at www.facebook.com/causes.

Keeping It Real

When you keep it real on Facebook, you're being authentic. Always strive to be in this frame of mind when you are talking to people on your Fan page. No one likes to be treated in a patronizing or pretentious manner, no matter the brand. We bring this up because we see this happen on Facebook a lot.

The voice of your business on Facebook is one that people will follow and see every day. Too many times, businesses will respond to comments on Facebook in too dry and monotone of a voice. Encourage your employees to show some personality. Give them the freedom to connect and bond to that individual who just reported she was having a problem.

Let's say a customer is having a rough time:

> Customer: "I'm having a really crappy day. Your site sucks. I haven't been able to access my account all day long and no one has gotten back to me since 9 A.M. this morning. It's now 5 P.M. I hate your company. —Ms. Alotta Whining"

Now a typical bureaucratic response would be something like this:

> You: "Ms. Whining. I'm sorry to hear that you are having an issue with your account. Are you sure you are typing in the right password? Please call our customer care center at 1-800-555-1212 where we'll be happy to get to the bottom of your issue. Hours are M–F, 9–5 P.M."

Can you see how impersonal this message is?

Here's how we recommend responding:

> You: "Alotta: I understand crappy days, it's been a crappy day here too with the site going down. Message me your phone number and I'll call you right now. I'll personally handle this for you and make sure you get squared away. —Your Name"

Can you see the difference? The first one is very canned and corporate and the other is very personal. With just a few modifications, you can go from canned and robotic to personal and caring.

Empathizing

It's important to relate to your fans with *empathy*. You need to remember that your Facebook Fan page isn't for you at all. It's for the fans who Like the page. Sure, you might own the page and can control what's posted on it, but the purpose of the page is so fans can communicate with a community of users who are interested in your business.

DEFINITION

Empathy denotes a deep emotional understanding of another person's feelings or problems.

Put yourself in their place when you think about the messages you post, and how you interact with them on a daily basis.

Here are some ways to get focused on fan empathy:

- **Listen to fans when they express their feelings.**

  Example: If a fan posts that the picture of the unicorn you shared on your Fan page Wall reminds them of a simpler time when the world was carefree …

  Wrong response: "Unicorns are fairy tales."

  Right response: "I remember when life was carefree as a child, too."

- **Let them know what you can do to help.**

  Example: A fan posts that the toy they just bought their child was on a recall website.

  Wrong response: "Which website?"

  Right response: "I'm sorry to hear that. Let's connect and I'll get this resolved for you and anyone else that might have the same issue."

- **Don't get angry.**

  Example: A fan posts that your company is irresponsible for making this world a dangerous place by selling weapons.

  Wrong response: "Touché."

  Right response: "I'm sorry you feel that way. Even as someone who accepts weapons, I too get intimidated by weapons sometimes. I wish everyone used them only for defense."

You can communicate by replying on the Fan page itself, or by messaging them directly. In some instances, you may want to tell the user that you will message them off the Wall for a personal conversation. In your message, you can find out how you can resolve their issue privately.

Many of the messages that get on Facebook may be product- or service-related questions. Address each one as soon as you can to maintain a good standing with your fans.

Clarity = Power

When businesses are completely focused on their vision and mission, they have clarity and it shows.

A good example is Apple, a hugely successful business that makes consumer electronics. Apple focuses on style to reach its market. The products are not faster, cheaper, or better, but they are more stylish and innovative.

This type of clarity makes them the powerhouse in the consumer electronics industry. Does your business have this kind of clarity? What do you need to do in order to get there? Make sure you are clear about your company's mission in your Facebook Profile.

Authority Figures

Every now and then, in every industry, someone is deemed the authority. John Wooden is an authority of college basketball coaching. Martina Navratilova is an authority on women's tennis. Bill Gates is an authority on computer software. Warren Buffet is an authority on financial investing. And Jimmy Buffett is an authority on Margaritaville.

Authority is never given. It is taken.

You need to take the role of the authority figure in your industry and online on Facebook. When you establish yourself as an authority, people will follow. And that creates a fan base in a hurry.

As you start to share information with your fans, ask and answer questions, and talk about the issues of your industry, you become the authority figure. Sounds too easy, doesn't it? The reality is that very few people and businesses do this. You can be the first and make it count.

Let's say you are a motorcycle shop. You sell and repair motorcycles, ATVs, and scooters. You build a Facebook Fan page and start to post status messages asking fans what bikes they want to see in the shop, what bikes they are sick of seeing, and if they would like to have a bikini bike wash on July 4th. These kinds of topics will make fans interact and encourage nonfans to become fans.

As more people start to like your business on Facebook, they will tell their friends, and as they comment on your page they spread the word automatically. As the motorcycle shop talks about the topics that mean the most to its audience, they are seen as the source to go to and the shop's Facebook page will quickly become the place to find the information your fans need.

Influencers

It's important in social media marketing to make friends with the right people. And the right people are influencers. Influencers are people who can really make your Facebook marketing promotions soar. They range from local celebrities to the ones in Hollywood, and many people in between.

Let's say Bono (lead singer for U2) were to say on his Facebook page that his favorite food was Domino's Pizza. All of his fans might see that post and think to themselves, "If Bono likes it, I like it." Now that's influence!

Where do you find an influencer? They are many ways to find influencers for your Facebook marketing campaigns.

You can find them by doing searches on Google. You can reach out to local or national celebrities. And you can even contact people in the media.

Let's say you own a local sporting goods store in Wilmington, North Carolina. Your target market is people that live or want to live an active lifestyle by exercising or playing sports. You can use Google to search for terms like, "sports Wilmington," "baseball Wilmington," and "surfing Wilmington." You'll want to filter the search results by displaying news, blogs, or discussions separately. This will help you identify the most popular sites and people that talk about your topic in your geographic area.

If you have a dentist office, you could do what a business did in my town that reached out to a local football star/customer and asked to use his name in their ads. The football star, William "The Refrigerator" Perry, was so flattered that he said "yes."

If you have a photography business that focuses on weddings, you may want to focus on finding the people in the community that have the most exposure to the wedding industry. This could be the local churches, dress shops that carry wedding dresses, shoe stores, and flower shops.

It is through these other businesses and resources that you will be able to find the right influencer(s), friend them in person or on Facebook, and utilize their position to reach more people.

High Integrity

The most influential aspect of any business success lies in its integrity. As a Facebook marketer, you are creating rapport daily in your posts, conversations, and interactions with your fans.

Here are some principles you should consider to really promote a high integrity and trustful environment in your organization:

- Recognize that customers want to do business with companies they can trust.

- If a project goes wrong, go above and beyond to redeem your company's brand. If it survives, you have stuck to your word. If it fails, you have peace that you did everything within your power.

- Train your team so that they are aligned with what you expect and make integrity part of your company culture. You must all be on the same page for this to work well.

It's so important that the voice and people who manage your social media marketing have high integrity. There is a huge amount of distrust online because people don't know the people they are talking to.

> **WATCH OUT**
>
> There is nothing worse in business than lying to your customers. It will bite you back hard if you get caught. Don't do it. Start from the top of the organization and institute a mission statement that focuses on ethics.

What they do experience firsthand is the way you talk to them, your tone of voice, and your approach.

Let's say you own an online music store and you have just promoted a 25 percent off sale on your Fan page for all products. Your fine print says that the products must be purchased by 5 P.M. The next morning you come into the office and you have over 100 orders that processed after 5 P.M. on the East Coast, but before 5 P.M. on the West Coast—and you have 100 emails from those 100 orders that say the website didn't take 25 percent off. What do you do?

Since you didn't clarify a time zone where the promotion ended, you should probably extend that 5 P.M. all the way to the West Coast. That would be the right thing to do. And in the future, be sure to note what time zone your deadlines are in when you post specials.

All You Need Is Love

I always end my speaking engagements with this phrase. "All you need is love; we are all social beings." This is the secret formula that makes social media marketing work for individuals and businesses, no matter how big they are now.

Here is the reason why love is important on Facebook:

- Everyone wants to be loved.
- Facebook loving is bigger than a Like any day.
- Love is about caring and sharing.
- Love is an individual choice.
- Love is the selfless promotion of your fans.

There is no Love link or button on Facebook, only the Like link. But if you aim high—really high—you may just hit the Like with flying colors.

If your prospective fans are not ready for love, will they consider Liking your business?

I Like You a Lot

Do you remember your first love? Probably. But do you remember your first like? Most people don't.

It might have been a GI Joe with the Kung Fu grip, Lincoln logs, Rock'em Sock'em Robots, a slinky dog, an Etch A Sketch, or a Radio Flyer wagon—brands that have stuck in our minds for years.

The same happens on Facebook. After people Like you, they may forget you unless you give them something to love about your business.

How do you do that on Facebook? You've got to have dialogue with people and poll them.

Let's say you own a kayak store, and you do rentals and tours. You've started a Facebook Fan page and you have 500 fans, but it's been the same 500 people for the last year. Yeah, it's a good group of regulars, but it's just not growing.

Another one of your hobbies is photography. One night you decide to take the camera out and photograph the stars from your kayak. You do a time lapse and create a video out of the photos over a period of 4 hours. You post this to your Facebook page that night and go to bed.

The next morning when you wake up, your fans have grown from 500 to 2,500. Not only has the number of people grown, but they are all talking about the photos and sharing the link to the photos with all of their friends. Topics on your Fan page turn from just being about kayaks to astronomy, photography, film, and hot dates. Your business and your Fan page just went from a like to a love.

People will only take like to the next level if emotion is involved. You need to excite and inspire people for them to love your business.

It Takes Time and Commitment

Getting people to love your Fan page is going to take some time and constant effort. It's not necessarily going to happen overnight with a single campaign.

Make sure you give yourself a realistic time period—at least three months—before you evaluate the performance of your Facebook marketing. Six months is an even better time period depending on the amount of effort you put into your campaigns. After one full year, you should be rocking out to Facebook marketing and achieving a large fan base with an interactive audience.

It's also going to take a strategic plan, the right training for your team, and being immersed in Facebook marketing and actions with the right voice and presence. The great thing is that you should now have the tools to put all of these together.

Within your Facebook marketing plan, objectives and platforms will change and you will need to adjust. Remain agile enough to do this—because it is certain that Facebook will change.

Love Is Patient, Love Is Kind

Your objective is to get fans to love your business on Facebook. You already know that this is going to take some time, but don't fret; get going right now, as soon as you put down this book.

All of the tips in this book will help you gain an edge over many other businesses on Facebook that simply fly by the seat of their pants and perform ad-hoc marketing. And in order to really gain the attention of fans and become that likeable and loveable source, be kind.

Kindness is the only thing that has ever changed the world.

The Least You Need to Know

- Great products and services help influence people to like a business, but it's the sensory aspects of the people behind the business that really make the business likeable.
- At the heart of the social web is a giving community.
- With just a few slight modifications, you can go from robotic to friendly conversation in a tone that matches the customer. Be empathetic, not sympathetic, to unsatisfied customers.
- Find influencers by combing media, including TV, radio, and blogs.
- Start from the top of the organization and create an ethical foundation.
- Make sure you give yourself a realistic three-month period before you evaluate your performance with Facebook marketing.

Glossary

ad   Short for advertisement, a piece of media—usually in print, online, or broadcast—that highlights a particular product or service.

admin   The administrator for your site. This person has control over your Facebook page. He or she can add, delete, or modify any information on the page. These duties can be shared among multiple people, but the power is usually limited to prevent too many conflicts.

app   Short for application, a software tool that works in conjunction with Facebook to deliver new functionality not found natively in Facebook.

blog   A website that features short articles, called posts, listed in order from newest to oldest. A blog can have professional content from, say, a daily newspaper, or posts from the average Joe or Jane.

campaign   A systematic course of aggressive activities used to attain more Likes for your Fan page. These Likes translate into existing and potential clients. It can also be described as a group of ads.

Chat   Using the computer to send messages with another person. Unlike email, which has a time delay, chat allows communication in real time. Chat services are also called instant messengers. Facebook Chat allows users to talk with other friends online within the website.

check-in   When a customer uses a mobile device to let friends know that he or she is visiting a particular establishment. Checking in is done via a social network, such as Facebook, or a check-in app, like FourSquare. The check-in is shared with the customer's friends, if not the general public, which creates advertising opportunities for the business.

check-in deal   A discount or bonus given to customers when they come to a particular venue or event. *See also* check-in.

click-through   When a user clicks on a link or an advertisement; the result is a recordable measurement.

click-through rate (CTR)   The number of clicks an ad received divided by the number of times it was shown.

comment   Leaving a message or a response to an online post. Customers may be more apt to follow a product line if they are given opportunities to comment, while comments in the right online conversation may get a business or service recognized by the public.

cost per click (CPC)   Fee system for online advertising in which you're charged on a per-click basis, meaning a user has to physically click on an ad before you are charged.

cost per impression (CPM)   Fee system for online advertising in which you're charged an agreed-upon fee each time an ad is loaded and displayed per group of 1,000 people. This is a passive measurement with the aim of getting more visibility.

credits   Currency used within Facebook. The website automatically translates users' real-life money into credits usable for Facebook purchases.

customer relationship management (CRM)   Software that enables you to keep track of your customers and prospects to help attract, engage, and maintain relationships.

dashboard   A high-impact visualization of statistical data that shows the performance of your particular product so you can make more informed decisions.

Deals   Any sale opportunity offered by a business. Facebook offers many opportunities for deals, from discounts for "Liking" a particular page to sales for people who check in through Facebook Mobile.

Event   A gathering set for a specific time through Facebook. It could be a real-life event, like a grand opening or a walk-in sale, or a virtual event, like a webinar or a product launch. Facebook allows users to set the date, time, and description of events, and will remind users of the event after they RSVP.

Facebook Ad Manager   The section of Facebook where you can create, edit, and delete ads and run performance reports on your ad campaigns.

fan   Someone who publicly says that he or she Likes a particular Facebook Fan page. Once the page is Liked, the fan is notified when the page is updated.

Fan page   A Facebook website dedicated to a particular person, place, business, or product. It gives Facebook users the opportunity to not only declare their interest in the subject, but to get the latest news as the page is updated by the owners. Fan pages aren't mutual, meaning that the business doesn't have to be friends with the fan in order for the fan to Like the Fan page.

friend   Someone who is interested in following the latest news on a brand or personal Profile. Friendships have to be accepted, so people always need to be asked if they want to be friends. Friendships must also be mutual, meaning that it is impossible for one person to be friends with someone who isn't his or her friend back.

frienemy   A competing person or company that you decide to work with, usually in a limited or carefully defined fashion. Both parties are usually aware that they can end the relationship at any time.

geotargeting   A method of determining the location of a website visitor and delivering targeted messages based on their location.

Group   A collection of users that are interested in a particular topic.

impressions   The number of times an ad or page was displayed.

influencer   Someone whose voice and actions other people in the community respect. Let's say Bono (lead singer for U2) were to say on his Facebook page that his favorite food was Domino's Pizza. All of his fans might see that post and think to themselves, "If Bono likes it, I like it."

Insights   Facebook reporting tool that measures users' activity on your Fan page. It provides statistics on user demographics, Likes, and shares that occur on your Facebook page.

lifetime Likes   The total number of people that have Liked your page.

Like   Public acknowledgment that a user is interested in a particular page featuring a person, product, event, or story. Like options often appear on websites, and a person's Likes are highlighted on his or her Facebook page.

LinkedIn   The largest professional social networking website with over 120 million users from around the world. The focus on LinkedIn is to network to find jobs, partners, and clients.

member   A person who is part of a Fan or Group page.

message   An email sent to a particular individual or group of individuals. Facebook allows messages between friends, between groups of friends, and to members of Group pages.

meta tag   Information inserted into the programming on your website.

News Feed   A chronological listing of Facebook statuses among friends.

niches   Subsets of a target market segment.

Notes   A notice posted on a Group page. Group members are notified when a new note is posted. Unlike messages, which are sent directly to members, Notes appear on the Facebook page itself.

organic shares   A metric that shows how many people shared your site link with others.

page   A Facebook website that has a person or business's information, pictures, and links. The page can also feature the Facebook Wall, an ongoing chronicle of the individual or company's interactions with others. The amount of information viewed by visitors can be controlled within the privacy settings.

Places   A Facebook service that allows customers to check in at a particular business or venue and show their location on their Facebook page. Customers must have Facebook Mobile on their phone to use Facebook Places. By allowing Facebook Places check-ins, businesses can get free advertising.

post   A note attached to a Profile. It's usually longer than a status update, providing extensive text, video, or pictures.

Profile   The Facebook page of a person, product, or brand. It can show various statistics, including the day of birth or creation, pictures, videos, and contact information.

pull marketing   Type of marketing in which individuals provide you with personal information.

push marketing   Any kind of marketing that gets users to go somewhere like a website or Fan page for information or a special.

ROI   Return on investment. Money gained or lost on your investment.

search engine optimization (SEO)   The process of organizing your web presence so Google, Yahoo!, and other search engines can find you easily. The better your SEO, the higher up on the list your brand will appear when someone searches for your business by name or keywords that describe your business.

segmentation   The process of dividing people into geographic, demographic, socioeconomic, psychographic, behavioral, and product categories. Segmentation makes it much easier to target your ideal audience.

social click-through rate (social CTR)   The number of social clicks divided by the number of social impressions.

social clicks   The total number of clicks your ad received that contained a viewer's friend(s) who Liked your page, event, or app.

social media policy   Statement outlining what is acceptable online behavior for a business. It's intended to protect the company and the employees from legal and social repercussions.

social media technology   Any software program that allows a user to communicate online with another user.

social media workflow   The process and system of who does what in a specific order within your social media marketing.

social network   A website that enables people to connect with like-minded individuals and to support and learn about their favorite brand. Facebook is a social network.

social percentage   Percentage of impressions where the ad was shown with information about a viewer's friend(s) who connected to your page.

Sponsored Stories   Advertisements that display recent interactions from viewers' friends with brands on Facebook.

status   A brief note attached to a Profile. It usually tells what is important to a person, company, or brand at the moment.

target market   The people who are most likely to buy from you.

Video   A movie posted on Facebook. Users can either use a webcam to record directly onto Facebook or provide a link to a YouTube video. Facebook embeds the video so users can view it without leaving the website.

Wall   A public place where a user or business can post items or receive commentary from others. Users can limit who or what can be posted on their Walls by adjusting the privacy settings.

Resources

This book is an excellent primer for successfully marketing your business on Facebook, but the website's evolving nature means that there is always new information out there. Here are our recommendations for online resources as well as other books to get you all the information you need.

Books

Social Media Marketing

Abernethy, Jennifer. *The Complete Idiot's Guide to Social Media Marketing.* Indianapolis: Alpha Books, 2010.

Baer, Jay, and Amber Naslund. *The NOW Revolution: 7 Shifts to Make Your Business Faster, Smarter and More Social.* New York: Wiley, 2011.

Brogan, Chris, and Julien Smith. *Trust Agents: Using the Web to Build Influence, Improve Reputation, and Earn Trust.* New York: Wiley, 2010.

Jaffe, Joseph. *Flip the Funnel: How to Use Existing Customers to Gain New Ones.* New York: Wiley, 2010.

Rowse, Barren, and Chris Garrett. *ProBlogger: Secrets for Blogging Your Way to a Six-Figure Income.* New York: Wiley, 2010.

Stelzner, Michael A. *Launch: How to Quickly Propel Your Business Beyond the Competition.* New York: Wiley, 2011.

Stratten, Scott. *UnMarketing: Stop Marketing. Start Engaging.* New York: John Wiley and Sons, 2010.

Facebook

Kirkpatrick, David. *The Facebook Effect: The Inside Story of the Company That Is Connecting the World*. New York: Simon & Schuster, 2011.

Kraynak, Joe, and Mikal E. Belicove. *The Complete Idiot's Guide to Facebook*. Indianapolis: Alpha Books, 2010.

Viral Media

Gunders, John, and Damon Brown. *The Complete Idiot's Guide to Memes*. Indianapolis: Alpha Books, 2010.

Scott, David Meerman. *The New Rules of Marketing and PR: How to Use Social Media, Blogs, News Releases, Online Video, and Viral Marketing to Reach Buyers Directly*. New York: Wiley, 2010.

Websites

eRocketFuel
erocketfuel.com

The social media marketing company of *The Complete Idiot's Guide to Facebook Marketing* co-author John Wayne Zimmerman.

DamonBrown.net
damonbrown.net

Writings of *The Complete Idiot's Guide to Facebook Marketing* co-author Damon Brown.

Social Media Examiner
SocialMediaExaminer.com

An online magazine dedicated to understanding social media.

Mashable
Mashable.com

From Silicon Valley, Mashable has the pulse on the next social media development.

All Facebook

AllFacebook.com

The most important Facebook website not created by Facebook. It has the latest website gossip, important news, and evolving trends.

Inside Facebook

InsideFacebook.com

A trend website geared toward Facebook developers, merchants, and businesses. A must-read for Facebook-based entrepreneurs and advertisers.

Facebook and the Social Media Playing Field

Facebook may be the most significant social network, but it certainly isn't the only game in town. Here is info on Facebook, competing websites, and why they all matter.

When and how did Facebook begin?

Harvard University students Mark Zuckerberg, Eduardo Saverin, Dustin Moskovitz, and Chris Hughes founded the website in 2004. Created in their dorm rooms, Facebook was essentially a living yearbook that enabled students to connect with each other. In fact, for the first couple of years, Facebook required all members to have an email address ending in .edu.

Facebook focused on Harvard students, but Zuckerberg and his colleagues quickly realized that it could be a connection between universities, too. Stanford University was one of the first major schools Facebook connected with outside of Harvard. Nestled in Silicon Valley, Stanford got Facebook serious attention from the tech community. Zuckerberg eventually moved to Silicon Valley and assumed total control over Facebook in a very controversial breakup. His former colleague and friend Saverin successfully sued him for part ownership of the website.

How many visitors does Facebook have?

It has more than 800 million users, with almost 500 million unique website visitors daily. Nearly 50 percent of America is on Facebook, and more than 70 percent of American web users are on Facebook.

How much is Facebook worth?

As of June 2011, Facebook is valued at $100 billion. It earned an estimated $2 billion in 2010.

Is Facebook the only social network?

Hardly. There are more than 100 social networks on the web.

What exactly does a social network do?

A social network enables people to connect with like-minded individuals and to support and learn about their favorite brands.

What social networks are similar to Facebook?

There are several, but the most important ones include these:

- **LinkedIn (www.linkedin.com):** LinkedIn is geared toward corporate and entrepreneurial people. It makes it easy to get referrals from others for jobs as well as providing introductions between two business contacts.

- **MySpace (www.myspace.com):** Once the largest social network, MySpace still commands 33 million regular users. It has been a favorite spot for teens and musicians, the latter becoming even more prominent after singer Justin Timberlake invested in it in 2011.

- **Orkut (www.orkut.com):** Now owned by Google, Orkut was launched before Facebook and has a similar feel. It hasn't made much of a splash in America, but it has more than 66 million users concentrated in India and Brazil.

- **Plaxo (www.plaxo.com):** Like LinkedIn, Plaxo is used often in the corporate world. Its big strength is the ability to organize all of your various contacts, on email or other mediums, in one place.

Isn't Twitter a social network?

Not really. It's a blogging platform that enables people to post messages. Although Twitter allows you to subscribe, or "follow," certain people, it doesn't have the more robust features of a social network like Profile pages, Wall posts, or group messaging.

That said, Twitter is still a valuable resource for businesses that want to create a constant presence and voice for the public.

Besides social networks, what else should I have in my online marketing plan?

We see six parts to the social media marketing field:

- Search
- Communities
- Email
- Social networks
- Reputation monitoring
- Blogs

Search is how easily people can find your brand online. The more easily you can be found, the better your search qualities. Much broader than social networks, communities can be developed in different environments. For instance, you can cultivate a community of people who connect online as well as in person. Email is one of the oldest online marketing mediums, and it enables you to directly contact individual customers. Reputation monitoring is actively searching the web to find out what customers think of your product, service, or brand. Finally, blogs give companies the opportunity to connect with tastemakers, and customers the chance to interact with their favorite brands.

Should I focus on a particular online marketing platform?

It's okay to put most of your energy toward, say, the music-friendly social network MySpace if you're going after performers, but a smart marketing plan always takes advantage of all six mediums in some form. Just be careful not to overextend your marketing commitment. You don't want to do them all if it causes you to do them all poorly. Take on what makes sense for your organization.

Your Facebook Marketing Checklist

Ready to open up your virtual doors on Facebook, but feel like you're forgetting something? Run down this checklist and make sure you didn't forget anything!

First Steps

- ❏ Map out your main goals with the Facebook page.
- ❏ Determine your main target audiences.
- ❏ Prioritize your goals and target audiences, and then organize your plan based on order of importance.
- ❏ Decide on the Facebook marketing voice you'd like to have on your page.
- ❏ Recognize competition that you may want to collaborate with in the future.

Next Steps

- ❏ Plan your campaign with the goal, the vehicles, the message, and the result.
- ❏ Decide between a Fan page and a Group page.
- ❏ Consider the balance between broadcast (news items) and interaction (call and response).
- ❏ View competitors' Fan and Group pages and steal their best ideas.

Advanced Steps

❐ Look into viral videos, games, and other methods of engagement.

❐ Use Facebook Analytics to see what has (and hasn't) been working.

❐ Add an e-commerce link to your page.

❐ Consider running promotions like contests and sweepstakes.

❐ Explore Facebook advertising.

❐ Investigate working with a Facebook consultant or social media agency.

Index